The Cotsw[...]
A practical Guide and S[...]

C000199355

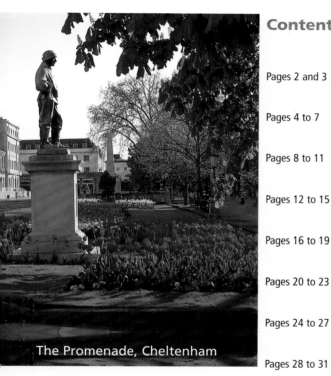

The Promenade, Cheltenham

Contents

Introduction

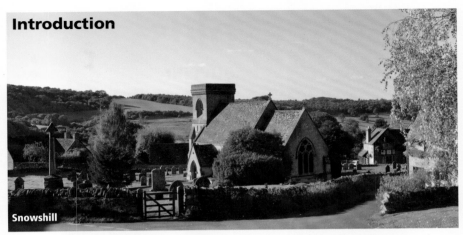

Snowshill

For some the name 'Cotswolds' conjures a picture of sheltered valleys harbouring villages of honey coloured stone nestling beside clear, fast flowing streams. Others may see the high, bleak open countryside criss-crossed by dry stone walls, or perhaps the bustling old market towns with their fine perpendicular churches. All these views are united by stone; it is oolitic limestone that has created the underlying landscape of the Cotswolds and the buildings for which the area is famed.

STEEPED IN OVER 4000 YEARS OF HISTORY

On the western edge of the Cotswold escarpment is the 4000 year old Belas Knap, one of the finest long barrows in the country. Its skilfully constructed dry stone walls are the earliest evidence of stonemasonry in an area known for the quality and hue of its stone.

The Romans established a military zone here, serviced by routes built with stone, some of those remaining are still followed by today's highways. A grass grown amphitheatre and a museum of Roman treasures remind us of the importance of the market town of Cirencester in former times. The Anglo Saxons left little evidence of their rule, other than a legacy of place-names and a few stone churches tucked away in quiet valleys, such as that in the tiny hamlet of Coln Rogers.

THE GOLDEN AGE OF THE COTSWOLDS

Following the Norman conquest of 1066 the church increased in power and wealth, built upon a thriving wool industry. By Domesday in 1086, most of the present day villages existed and an open field system had been created, with vast flocks of sheep grazing on the open sheep walk.

Today's market towns, such as Chipping Campden and Northleach, were founded at this time, built of local stone with the help of masonry skills brought with the Normans. By the 15th century the whole country was so dependent on the wool industry that the Lord Chancellor's seat in the House of Lords came to be known as the woolsack. The Cotswolds thrived upon the wool trade; wealthy merchants built fine houses and elegant perpendicular churches. Wool processing became increasingly important to the economy; it was initially a cottage industry, but during the 16th century the weaving and fulling became concentrated in the towns and villages of the western Cotswolds where the fast flowing streams from the steep slopes powered the mills.

Pour beaucoup les 'Cotswolds' sont un pays de vallées encaissées abritant des villages de pierre dorée construits sur les berges de rivières aux eaux claires et vives.

Pour d'autres ce sont de hauts plateaux ouverts aux vents et quadrillés de murs de pierres sèches ou encore de vieilles villes commerçantes animées avec leurs églises de style Perpendiculaire.

C'est la pierre qui donne son unité à toutes ces images, car c'est le calcaire tendre oolithique qui est à l'origine du paysage des Cotswolds et des bâtiments qui font la renommée de cette région.
ENRACINEE DANS PLUS DE 4000 ANS D'HISTOIRE

Perché sur l'extrémité ouest du relief escarpé des Cotswolds se trouve Belas Knap, un des plus beaux tumulus de tout le pays, vieux de 4000 ans.

La pierre locale a été utilisée par les romains pour construire leurs routes militaires, dont certaines subsistent encore et sont empruntées par les routes d'aujourd'hui. Un amphithéâtre recouvert d'herbe et un musée des trésors romains nous rappellent l'importance de la ville commerçante animée de Cirencester dans le passé. Les Anglo-saxons ont laissé peu de traces de leur domination sauf un patrimoine de noms de lieux et quelques églises en pierre.
L'AGE D'OR DES COTSWOLDS

Lors du premier cadastral recensement en 1086 la plupart des villages actuels existaient déjà et un paysage de prairies ouvertes avait déjà été crée pour faire paître de vastes troupeaux de moutons. Les Cotswolds s'enrichirent grâce au commerce de la laine ; de riches

marchands construisirent des maisons raffinées et d'élégantes églises de style Perpendiculaire telles que St Peter and St Paul a Northleach et l'église St Mary's a Chipping Norton. Le travail de la laine devint de plus en plus important pour l'économie et pendant le 16eme siècle le tissage et le foulage se concentrèrent dans les villes et les villages de l'ouest des Cotswolds, avec ses pentes accentuées et ses torrents.
REDECOUVERTE

Entre 1700 et 1840 la concurrence conduisit à un déclin brutal et la région souffrit durement de sa dépendance de l'activité lainière, mais au 19eme siècle William Morris, entre autres, prit conscience du riche héritage architectural du 15eme et 16eme siècle et de cet intérêt naquit l'Association pour la Protection des Anciens Bâtiments. A partir de ce moment les visiteurs affluèrent, attirés non pas par la majesté de grands bâtiments, mais par les fermes et les cottages empreints d'Histoire, par les églises paroissiales et les petites villes commerçantes riches de leur passé et c'est sans doute cela qui est typique des Cotswolds d'aujourd'hui.

EINFÜHRUNG

Für manchen birgt der Name „Cotswolds" ein Bild von malerischen Dörfern aus honigfarbenem Stein, durchflossen von kristallklaren gurgelnden Bächen, eingebettet in schützende Täler. Andere mögen die hohe, rauhe offene Landschaft sehen, kreuz und quer durchzogen von Bruchsteinmauern, oder vielleicht die geschäftigen historischen Marktstädtchen mit ihren prächtigen Kirchen, errichtet im perpendicular style. Alle diese Ansichten werden geprägt vom typischen Cotswold-Stein, einem oolithischen Kalkstein, der sowohl die Landschaft der Cotswolds als auch die Bauwerke geformt hat für die diese Gegend so berühmt ist.
DURCHDRUNGEN VON MEHR ALS 4000 JAHREN GESCHICHTE

Auf der westlichen Kante der Cotswold-Erhebung befindet sich Belas Knap, ein 4000 Jahre altes Hügelgrab, das als eines der eindrucksvollsten des Landes gilt.

Einige der von den Römern aus lokalem Stein gebauten Militärstraßen bestehen noch heute in ihrem Verlauf als Landstraßen. Ein von Gras überwuchertes Amphitheater und ein Museum mit römischen Schätzen erinnert uns an die Bedeutung des geschäftigen Marktfleckens Cirencester in vergangenen Zeiten. Die Angelsachsen hinterließen wenige Zeichen ihrer Herrschaft, abgesehen von Ortsnamen und einigen steinernen Kirchen.
DAS GOLDENE ZEITALTER DER COTSWOLDS

Zur Zeit des Domesday im Jahre 1086 existierte bereits die Mehrheit der heutigen Dörfer, und es war ein System von offenen Feldern für

REDISCOVERY

Between 1700 and 1840, parliamentary intervention, higher taxation and an increase in wool production elsewhere, led to a decline in the Cotswold wool industry and the area paid for an over reliance on the trade. Ironically the rich legacy of 15th and 16th century buildings we see today is partly due to this period of poverty, as there was little money available for new building, although a wealthy minority did build several substantial country houses.

The Cotswolds is unusual for the range and quality of its stone buildings, from the cottages and churches of local communities to larger manor houses. Towards the end of the 19th century the value of these buildings was noticed by several well meaning philanthropists, including William Morris. They recognised the unique architectural unity and wealth of the area, setting up the Society for the Protection of Ancient Buildings. From the early 19th century visitors began to come here, not for the grandeur of large buildings but for the living history of farms and cottages, parish churches and small market towns. It is perhaps this that most characterises the Cotswolds of today, a sense that the buildings are from, as well as part of the landscape.

große Schafsherden geschaffen worden. Die Cotswolds florierten durch den Wollhandel. Wohlhabende Händler errichteten prächtige Häuser, sowie elegante Kirchen im perpendicular style, wie zum Beispiel St. Peter und Paul in Northleach und St. Mary's in Chipping Norton. Die Wollverarbeitung gewann zunehmend an Bedeutung für die Wirtschaft, und während des 16. Jahrhunderts konzentrierten sich Webereien und Walkereien in den Städten und Dörfern der westlichen Cotswolds mit ihren steilen Hängen und schnell-fließenden Bächen.

DIE WIEDERENTDECKUNG

Zwischen 1700 und 1840 führte Konkurrenz zu einer starken Rezession, und die Region musste schwer für ihre Abhängigkeit von der Wolle bezahlen. Im 19. Jahrhundert erkannten William Morris und andere jedoch das reiche Erbe an Bauwerken aus dem 15. und 16. Jahrhundert, und dieses Interesse führte zur Gründung der Gesellschaft zum Schutz Historischer Bauwerke. Seit dieser Zeit kamen die Besucher nicht wegen der Mächtigkeit der großen Bauwerke, sondern wegen der lebendigen Geschichte der Farmen und Cottages, Pfarrkirchen und kleinen Marktflecken hierher. Das ist es vermutlich auch, was die Cotswolds von heute am meisten kennzeichnet.

はじめに

「コッツウォルズ」という名前に、ある人は、ほとばしる清流のほとりに建つハチ蜜色をした石壁や石垣をもつ家の並ぶ谷間の村のイメージを思い浮かべます。また、石垣が縦横に走る荒涼とした丘陵や、美しい尖塔をもつ教会とにぎやかな古い市場のある町を思い浮かべる人もいます。これらの風景をつなぐのが「石」です。コッツウォルズの景観を生んだ石、有名なコッツウォルズの石造りの家に使われている石 は魚卵状石灰岩といいます。

4000 年の歴史を追って

コッツウォルド丘陵の西側の崖には、「ベラス ナップ」と呼ばれる 4000 年前の石造りの古墳があります。これは英国で最も有名な古墳の 1 つです。

古代ローマ人は、地元の石を使ってその軍事道路を建設しました。現在のハイウェイ網の基にもなっているこれらのローマ街道の一部は今日でも見ることができます。草の茂る円形劇場やローマ時代の宝物を展示した博物館が、現在商業都市としてにぎわう「サイレンセスター」の過去の姿を彷彿とさせてくれます。その後、この地を支配したアングロ サクソン人は、地名と石造りの教会のほかには、遺跡をほとんど残していません。

コッツウォルズの黄金時代

1086 年のノルマン人の検地帳「ドゥームズデー ブック」の記録によると、今日の村の大部分と大量の羊の群れを放牧するための開放耕地制があったことがわかります。コッツウォルズは羊毛貿易によって繁栄し、富裕な商人によって、ノースリーチのセント ピーター教会やセント ポール教会、チッピング ノートンのセント マリー教会などの優雅な尖塔をもつ教会や、瀟洒な住宅が建てられました。16 世紀には、羊毛加工業の経済的重要性が増し、急峻な丘と清流の多いコッツウォルズ西部の町や村には、毛織物工場や縮充工場が集まっていました。

コッツウォルズの再発見

1700 年から 1840 年にかけて、毛織物に大きく依存していたコッツウォルズは産業構造の変化に取り残され、急速に衰退していきました。しかし、19 世紀の後半にはウィリアム・モリスをはじめとする文化人により、15～16 世紀の豊かな建築遺産が再評価され、古代建築保護委員会が設立されました。これ以降、コッツウォルズには、壮大な建造物ではなく、生きた歴史を伝える牧場や農家、教区教会や小さな市場町が織り成す魅力を求めて人々が訪れるようになりました。そして、これが今日のコッツウォルズの魅力でもあります。

Chipping Campden

Chipping Campden, at the northern end of the Cotswold Way, first became a borough market in the 12th century, the name 'Chipping' means market.

The High Street was lined with small shops on long narrow burgage plots running back to service lanes. Although this layout remains, stone buildings from the 14th century onward replaced the original wooden structures. The town had flourished with the profits from wool, but the decline of the wool industry brought poverty. In the early 20th century a 'Guild of Handicrafts' was established, it only lasted a few years but its legacy and influence remain in the range of outlets specialising in the creative arts. The Campden Trust was also set up, helping to preserve the town's many historic buildings.

Today the rich golden hues of Cotswold stone from northern quarries are still evident in the town and Chipping Campden remains a leading centre for visitors, with excellent local facilities.

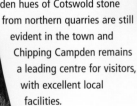

■ **TIC High Street, Chipping Campden. 01386 841206**

ATTRACTIONS, EVENTS, AND POINTS OF INTEREST
■ Ernest Wilson Memorial Garden – Open all year – dedicated to the renowned Victorian plant collector.
■ The Silk Mill – Open all year – houses working gold and silversmiths, an Art gallery and a Cafe

■ Dover's Hill Games – held the weekend after Spring Bank Holiday. Sir Robert Dover founded them during the reign of James I. The hill, a National Trust site, affords splendid views over the Avon Valley.
■ The Market Hall dates from 1627.
■ The ruins of Old Campden House, once the home of Sir Baptist Hicks – destroyed by fire during the English Civil War 1642 to 1646 – lie on the edge of the town.
■ Parts of St James Church date from 13th, 14th and 15th centuries.

Chipping Campden à l'extrémité nord du Cotswold Way, devint une bourgade commerçante au 12ème siècle et son nom 'Chipping' signifie marché.

La ville avait prospéré grâce à la laine, et le déclin de l'industrie lainière y amena la pauvreté. Au début du vingtième siècle la Guilde de l'Artisanat fut créée ; elle ne dura que quelques années mais son influence se manifeste encore à travers l'abondance des magasins d'artisanat.

Le plan initial de la High Street est resté inchangé bien que les bâtiments de pierre aient remplacé les constructions d'origine en bois.

Aujourd'hui les riches tonalités dorées de la pierre des Cotswolds sont visibles sur ces bâtiments, dont certains remontent jusqu'au quatorzième siècle et Chipping Camden reste l'un des grands centres touristiques.

Chipping Campden, gelegen am Nordende des Cotswold Way, wurde erstmals im 12. Jahrhundert als Marktbezirk erwähnt. Der Name „Chipping" bedeutet soviel wie „Markt".

Florierte die Stadt einst von den Profiten der Wolle, so brachte der Niedergang der Wollindustrie Armut mit sich. Im frühen 20. Jahrhundert wurde eine Handwerkergilde gegründet. Obwohl sie nur wenige Jahre überdauerte, bestehen ihr Vermächtnis und Einfluss in einer Anzahl von Werkstätten des Kunsthandwerks fort.

Die ursprüngliche Anordnung der High Street ist bis heute erhalten geblieben, obwohl die ursprünglichen Holzstrukturen durch Steinbauten ersetzt wurden. Heute noch sind die kräftigen goldenen Farbtöne des Cotswold-Steins in diesen Gebäuden, die bis ins 14. Jahrhundert zurückreichen, sichtbar und Chipping Campden bleibt ein führendes Besucherzentrum.

12 世紀に自治都市の市場町として始まったチッピング キャムデンはコッツウォルド街道の北端にあります。「チッピング」とは「市場」の意味です。

チッピング キャムデンは毛織物工業の勃興とともに繁栄し、毛織物工業とともに衰退しました。20 世紀初頭には「手工芸品ギルド」が設立されました。このギルドは数年しか存続しませんでしたが、その伝統は現在もこの町に並ぶ創作工芸品の専門店に見ることができます。

この町の目抜き通り「ハイストリート」は、創建当時の木骨構造の家から石造りの家へと代わりましたが、街並みそのものは当時のままです。14 世紀までさかのぼることができる現在の建物には、クリーム色をしたコッツウォルドの石が使われています。今日のチッピング キャムデンは、昔日の市場のにぎわいを取り戻したかのようです。

Broadway

Broadway maintains much of the charm that attracted the Victorian artists and writers who first popularised it. A variety of 16th to 18th century golden Guiting stone buildings, from cottages to Georgian manors, line the wide grass-fringed 'broad way' leading from the foot of the western escarpment through the village. St Eadburgha's Church, about a mile from the busy main street, is of Norman origin but dates largely from the 15th century.

From about 1600 Broadway became a staging post on the route from London to Worcester, and at its busiest 33 Public Houses refreshed weary travellers and their horses. Most famous among the remaining inns is the Lygon Arms, purchased from General Lygon by his butler. The development of the railways led to a quieter period for Broadway, until it was 'discovered' by prominent Victorians such as William Morris, JM Barrie, Henry James, Vaughan Williams, John Singer Sargent and Frank Millett, who later died on the Titanic. Since that time the village has been a popular destination for visitors, attracted by the fine Cotswold architecture, hostelries and craft shops.

■ **TIC Unit 14, Russell Square, High Street, WR12 7AP Broadway. 01386 852937**

ATTRACTIONS, EVENTS, AND POINTS OF INTEREST
- Christmas Box – Open May to December. An Aladdins Cave of Christmas paraphernalia.
- Broadway Tower Country Park – Open April to October. Limited opening at other times – 01386 852390. An area of outstanding natural beauty, with views over 13 counties from a unique folly tower. Nature walks, café and shop.
- Edward Elgar and, in her early years, the Queen Mother were regular guests of Mary Anderson, the famous American actress, who lived in the High Street.
- The Cotswold Way passes through the village.

Broadway a conservé une grande partie du charme qui attiraient les artistes et les écrivains Victoriens qui l'ont popularisée. Un ensemble de bâtiments construits dans la pierre dorée de Guiting et datant du 16ème au 18ème siècle borde la large « Broadway ».

A partir de 1600 environ Broadway devint un relais sur la route de Londres à Worcester et à son apogée il y avait 33 pubs pour rafraîchir les voyageurs fatigués. La plus renommée des auberges qui subsistent est le Lygon Arms. Le développement du chemin de fer se traduisit par une période plus calme pour Broadway, jusqu'à sa « découverte » par les artistes et écrivains Victoriens tels que J.M. Barrie, Henry James, Vaughan Williams et Elgar, ainsi que William Morris. Depuis cette époque-là le village attire de nombreux visiteurs, grâce à son architecture raffinée caracteristique des Cotswolds, ses hôtels et ses magasins d'artisanat.

Broadway hat viel von seinem Charme beibehalten, der einst die viktorianischen Künstler und Schriftsteller, die es populär machten, anzog. Eine Vielfalt von Gebäuden, die zwischen dem 16. und 18. Jahrhundert aus dem goldenen Guiting-Stein errichtet wurden, säumt den breiten „Broadway".

Ab ca. 1600 war Broadway ein Rastplatz an der Hauptreiseroute von London nach Worchester. Zu den geschäftigsten Zeiten erfrischten 33 Wirtshäuser die müden Reisenden. Das berühmteste unter den verbliebenen Gasthäusern sind die Lygon Arms. Die Entwicklung der Eisenbahnen führte zu einer ruhigeren Zeit für Broadway bis es durch die viktorianischen Künstler und Schriftsteller, wie z.B. J.M. Barrie, Henry James, Vaughan Williams und Elgar, sowie William Morris wiederentdeckt wurde. Seit jener Zeit ist das Dorf ein beliebtes Ziel für Besucher, die von der prächtigen Cotswold- Architektur, den Wirtshäusern und den Kunstgewerbeläden angezogen werden.

ブロードウェイには、ここを再発見したビクトリア朝の芸術家や作家が紹介した当時の魅力が今も色濃く残っています。「ブロードウェイ」という名のとおり幅の広い通りには、ギッティング採石場産のクリーム色の石を使った 16 世紀から 18 世紀の建物が並んでいます。

ロンドンとウースターをつなぐ駅馬車が停まる宿場町として 1600 年代初頭に発達したこの町の最盛期には、旅人の疲れをいやすために 33 軒のパブが営業していました。今も残るこれらのパブの中で最も有名なのは、「ライゴン アームズ」(Lygon Arms) です。鉄道の発達に伴って、ブロードウェイは衰退しましたが、ビクトリア時代になって、J.M.バリー、ヘンリー・ジェームズ、ボーン・ウィリアムズ、エルガー、ウィリアム・モリスといった作家や芸術家たちによって再発見されました。このときから、よく保存されたコッツウォルズの建物、旅館、工芸品店などが、この村を訪れる旅人の目を楽しませてくれます。

Moreton-in-Marsh

The principal town of the northern Cotswolds, Moreton grew up in the 13th century as a market town on the busy Fosse Way. Its exceptionally wide main street lined by many elegant 18th century buildings still supports a thriving Tuesday market, and an annual one-day agricultural and horse show.

Moreton has long been associated with transport; there was a camp here when the Fosse Way was first built, and even then it probably offered a place for travellers to rest. Later it became a stopping place for stage-coaches on the route from London to Aberystwyth, until the coming of the Oxford to Worcester Railway in 1843. It is one of the few places in the Cotswolds to be served by a railway.

The oldest building now is probably the 16th century curfew tower; its bell rang out nightly until 1860 to remind people of the risk of fire at night. The fire fighting connection continues, with the fire service-training centre based near the town.

- ■ **TIC Cotswold District Council Offices. 01608 650881.**
- ■ **VIC St Edwards Hall, The Square, Stow On The Wold, GL54 1AF. 01451 870998**
- **ATTRACTIONS, EVENTS, AND POINTS OF INTEREST**
- ■ Market Day – Tuesday.
- ■ The Moreton Show, one of the biggest one-day agricultural and horse shows in the country, held on the first Saturday in September.
- ■ Wellington Aviation Museum – Open all year except Mondays – 01608 650323. Many interesting artefacts of aircraft and local history.

Ville principale du nord des Cotswolds, Moreton se développa au 13ème siècle en tant que ville commerçante sur la Fosse Way très passante. Sa grand-rue exceptionnellement large bordée d'élégantes maisons du 18ème siècle est encore occupée tous les mardi par un marché très actif et un salon annuel de l'agriculture et du cheval se tient en ville le premier samedi de septembre.

Moreton a longtemps été associée au développement du transport; il y avait un camp en ce lieu lors de la construction de la Fosse Way. Plus tard elle devint un arrêt apprécié sur la route de Londres à Aberystwyth pour les malles-postes, jusqu'à l'avènement de la ligne de chemin de fer d'Oxford à Worcester en 1843. C'est l'un des rares endroits des Cotswolds qui soit desservi par le chemin de fer.

Die wichtigste Stadt der nördlichen Cotswolds, Moreton, entwickelte sich im 13. Jahrhundert als ein Marktflecken am geschäftigen Fosse Way. In seiner außergewöhnlich breiten Hauptstraße mit ihren vielen eleganten Bauten aus dem 18. Jahrhundert wird noch heute jeden Dienstag ein florierender Markt abgehalten, und alljährlich findet am ersten Samstag im September in der Stadt eine eintägige Landwirtschafts- und Pferdeschau statt.

Moreton wird schon seit langer Zeit mit Transport assoziiert. Es gab hier bereits ein Zeltlager als der Fosse Way gebaut wurde. Später wurde der Ort ein beliebter Rastplatz für Postkutschen auf der Route von London nach Aberystwyth, bis zur Ankunft der Eisenbahnlinie von Oxford nach Worchester im Jahre 1843. Moreton ist einer der wenigen Orte in den Cotswolds, die an einer Eisenbahnlinie liegen.

モートン イン マーシュは、13 世紀にフォッス街道 (Fosse Way) 沿いの市場町として発達した北部コッツウォルズ第一の町です。18 世紀の建物が並ぶ広い目抜き通りでは、今日でも火曜日ごとに市場が立ちます。また、毎年 9 月の第 1 土曜日には、農産物と馬術ショーを中心とした祭りが開催されます。

モートン イン マーシュは、フォッス街道が初めて建設されたときローマ軍の駐屯地となり、その後は、1843 年にオックスフォードとウースター間に鉄道が敷設されるまで、ロンドンとウェールズのアベリストウィスとをつなぐ駅馬車の停まる宿場町として栄えました。モートン イン マーシュは、コッツウォルズで数少ない鉄道の駅がある町です。

Area 1 General

OTHER ATTRACTIONS IN AREA 1

Almonry Museum, Evesham – Open all year (closed for 2 weeks at Christmas) – 01386 446944 - a local history museum.

Batsford Arboretum, Batsford – Open all year – 01386 701441. Established in the 1880s by Lord Redesdale, an informal arboretum featuring oriental trophies and includes the unusual handkerchief tree. Also on site is Batsford Garden Centre – Open all year – 01386 700409.

Broadway Tower

Anne Hathaway's Cottage

Cotswold Falconry Centre, Batsford – Open March to November – 01386 701043. Daily 'Flying Displays' by eagles, hawks, owls and falcons. Contact: mark@cotswold-falconry.co.uk

Evesham Country Park, Evesham – Open all year. A 130-acre estate with Wildlife Visitor Centre, Coarse Fishing, Restaurant, Garden and Shopping Centre.

Hidcote Manor Garden, near Chipping Campden – Open February to October 01386 438333. Created by horticulturist Major Lawrence Johnston, really a series of small gardens, now a National Trust site. Licensed restaurant, plant centre and shop.

Kiftsgate Court, near Chipping Campden – Open April to September (call for opening times) – 01386 438777. Beautiful gardens in grounds of Georgian Manor GL55 6LN.

Mill Dene Garden, Blockley – Open April to October (Tuesday to Friday 10am - 5.30pm) 01386 700457. Privately owned gardens with many hidden pathways, tearoom and shop. GL56 9HU.

Shakespeare Birthplace Trust, Stratford – Open all year – 01789 204016. Includes Shakespeare's Birthplace, Anne Hathaway's Cottage, Mary Arden's House and other properties associated with the Bard.

Snowshill Manor, Snowshill – April to October phone for opening times 01386 852410. A Tudor Manor owned by the National Trust featuring a collection of crafts from around the world including Samurai armour, musical instruments and bicycles. WR12 7JU

OTHER PLACES OF INTEREST IN AREA 1

Stratford-upon-Avon, a major tourist centre, lies just 12 miles north of Chipping Campden. South along the foot of the escarpment are the villages of Mickleton, Willersey, Buckland, Stanton and Stanway. West is the vale of Evesham, a major fruit growing area centred on the market towns of Evesham and Pershore and dissected by the rivers Severn and Avon.

To the south of Chipping Campden lie Broad Campden and Blockley. The latter a delightful mix of 17th and 18th century houses built around prospering silk mills, sadly redundant today. South again, the pretty terraced houses of Bourton-on-the-Hill line the steep A44 with views towards Moreton-in-Marsh. Here the Norman church houses a rare survivor of old English standard measures, a beautiful bell metal Winchester Bushel and Peck, made in 1816. At the bottom of the hill are Batsford Arboretum and Sezincote.

OTHER TICs
- TIC The Almonry, Abbey Gate, Evesham. 01386 446944
- TIC 21 Church Street, Malvern. 01684 892289
- TIC Bridgefoot Stratford-upon-Avon. 01789 264293

Autres lieux intéressants – Région 1
 Stratford-upon-Avon, un centre touristique important, se trouve seulement à 20 km au nord de Chipping Campden. La route au sud traverse les villages de Mickleton, Willersey, Buckland, Stanton et Stanway, qui présentent tous les reflets dorés de la pierre des Cotswolds. A l'ouest dans la vallée d'Evesham coulent la Severn et l'Avon.
 Au sud de Chipping Campden on trouve les villages de Broad Campden et de Blockley. Ce dernier est un ensemble magnifique de maisons du 17ème et 18ème siècle bâties autour de filatures de soie autrefois prospères, malheureusement désaffectées de nos jours.
 Au sud encore Bourton-on-the-Hill aligne ses jolies maisons le long de la descente de la A44 vers Moreton-in-Marsh. L'église de style Normand abrite un des rares survivants des anciennes mesures anglaises, un magnifique boisseau métallique de Winchester, fabriqué en 1816. En bas de la colline s'étendent Batsford Arboretum et Sezincote.

Weitere Sehenswerte Orte – Gebiet 1
 Stratford-upon-Avon, ein bedeutendes Touristenzentrum, liegt nur 20 km nördlich von Chipping Campden. Die Straße nach Süden führt durch die Orte Mickleton, Willersey, Buckland, Stanton und Stanway, die alle die goldenen Farbtöne des Cotswold-Steins zeigen. Westlich, im Tal von Evesham, findet man die Flüsse Severn und Avon.
 Südlich von Chipping Campden liegen Broad Campden und Blockley. Letzteres ist eine reizende Mischung aus Häusern, die im 17. und 18. Jahrhundert zusammen mit florierenden Seidenspinnereien errichtet wurden, die heute leider außer Betrieb sind.
 Weiter südlich säumen die hübschen Reihenhäuser von Burton-on-the-Hill die steile Landstraße A44 nach Moreton-in-Marsh. Die normannische Kirche beherbergt ein seltenes Überbleibsel der alten englischen Standardmaße, einen herrlichen bronzenen Winchester Scheffel aus dem Jahre 1816. Am Fuße des Berges befinden sich das Batsford Arboretum und Sezincote.

その他の見どころ — エリア 1
 シェークスピアの生まれた町として名高いストラトフォード オン エーボン（Stratford-upon-Avon）は、チッピング カムデンから北へ 20 キロほどのところにあり、スタンウェイ（Stanway）、スタントン（Stanton）、バックランド（Buckland）、ウィラジー（Willersey）、ミックルトン（Mickleton）などのコッツウォルズの石造りの建物の並ぶ村々を通っていくことができます。西側のイーブシャムの谷にはセバーン川とエーボン川が流れています。
 チッピング カムデンの南には、ブロード カムデン（Broad Campden）とブロックリー（Blockley）があります。ブロックリーでは、すでに閉鎖された製糸工場を中心にした 17〜18 世紀の街並みが楽しめます。モートン イン マーシュの西側、A44 号線沿いの丘バートン オン ザ ヒル（Bourton-on-the-Hill）には美しいテラス ハウスのほか、ノルマン様式の教会があり、昔の計量単位であるブッシェルとペックの珍しい青銅製の升が残っています。丘のふもとにあるバッツフォード植物園（Batsford Arboretum）とセジンコット（Sezincote）も見どころです。

Gloucester

Situated beyond the western escarpment and beside the river Severn, Gloucester's greatest glory is its cathedral. An original Saxon monastery rebuilt from 1100, the oldest part remaining is the Chapter House where in 1085 William the Conqueror drew up his plans for the Domesday Book. Today's cathedral prides itself on being welcoming and embracing the 21st century, it is one of the chosen locations for the films of Harry Potter.

There are no remains of the original settlement, but the museum houses many artefacts of the Roman city of Glevum. Saxon Gloucester rivalled London in importance, becoming a key garrison city on the Wessex-Mercia border. The city was granted a port in 1580 by Elizabeth I; this thrived, reaching its peak in the early 19th century but declining with the advent of larger ships. The Victorian docks have been revitalised, the warehouses now occupied by museums, restaurants and offices, a vibrant place to visit.

■ TIC 28 Southgate Street, Gloucester, GL1 2DP
01452 396572

ATTRACTIONS, EVENTS, AND POINTS OF INTEREST
- Market Day – Indoor, Monday and Saturday Cattle, Monday and Thursday
- Farm Market at Over, open everyday
- Gloucester Antiques Centre – Open all year – 01452 529716. 100 individual dealers.
- Gloucester Cathedral – Open all year – 01452 528095. Ranked as one of England's most beautiful, it features the tomb of Edward II, world-famous fan-vaulted cloisters and medieval glass. Guided tours, restaurant and shop.
- Museum of Gloucester and Art Gallery and TIC – Open all year – 01452 396131. Includes Roman artefacts, dinosaur bones, the amazing Birdlip Mirror and hands on displays.
- Gloucester Life Museum – Open all year – 01452 396467. Includes local history, crafts and industry from 1500, a dairy and ironmongers shop, carpenter and wheelwright. Special events are held al year.
- Historic Inland Docks – Open all year. The furthest inland port in Britain. Boat trips can be taken from here along the Gloucester to Sharpness canal during the summer.
- Gloucester Waterways Museum – Open all year – An award-winning museum with many interactive exhibits and a working blacksmith.
- Soldiers of Gloucester Museum – Open all year – 01452 522682. Exhibits from 300 years of military history.
- Gloucester Festival – In July the streets and parks are full of entertainment for all the family.
- Robinswood Country Park - Superb views across the Severn Valley.

Située derrière l'escarpement ouest et à côté de la Severn, Gloucester tire sa renommée de sa glorieuse cathédrale. Le monastère saxon d'origine fut rebâti à partir de 1100 ; sa plus ancienne partie est la salle du chapître où en 1085 Guillaume le Conquérant établit ses plans pour le premier livre du cadastre.

Il ne reste rien de l'établissement d'origine mais le musée abrite beaucoup d'objets de la ville romaine de Glevum. La Gloucester saxonne rivalisa en importance avec Londres, devenant une place forte stratégique sur la frontière entre Wessex et Mercia. La ville fut dotée d'un port par Elizabeth I et atteignit son apogée au début du 19ème siècle. Les docks Victoriens ont été réhabilités et les entrepôts aménagés en musées, restaurants et bureaux ; cela mérite le détour.

Jenseits des Westhanges der Cotswolds am Fluss Severn liegt Gloucester, dessen größter Stolz seine Kathedrale ist. Das ursprüngliche angelsächsische Kloster wurde nach 1100 umgebaut, und der älteste noch bestehende Teil ist das Kapitelhaus wo Wilhelm der Eroberer im Jahre 1085 seine Pläne für das Domesday Book aufsetzte.

Von der ursprünglichen Siedlung sind keine Überreste erhalten, aber das Museum beherbergt viele Artefakte der römischen Stadt Glevum. Das angelsächsische Gloucester konnte sich in seiner Bedeutung mit London messen und wurde zu einer der wichtigsten Garnisonstädte an der Wessex-Mercia Grenze. Die Stadt, der 1580 von Elizabeth I das Hafenrecht zugesprochen wurde, erreichte seinen Höhepunkt im frühen 19. Jahrhundert. Die viktorianischen Docks wurden neu belebt, und die Speicher, die jetzt Museen, Restaurants und Büros beherbergen, lohnen einen Besuch.

コッツウォルド丘陵の西側を流れるセバーン川のほとりに広がるグロスターは荘厳な大聖堂で有名です。この大聖堂は、もともとはサクソン人の修道院でしたが、1100 年以降改築されました。現存する最も古い建物であるチャプター ハウス（Chapter House）は、1085 年に征服王ウィリアムが検地帳「ドゥームズデー ブック」の構想を練ったことで知られています。

最初の町の遺跡は残っていませんが、ローマ時代の植民都市グレブム（Glevum）から出土した多くの遺物が博物館に陳列されています。サクソン時代のグロスターはロンドンと並ぶ重要な町で、ウェセックス王国とマーシア王国の国境地帯の軍事的に重要な都市になりました。1580 年には、女王エリザベス 1 世により、港湾施設をもつことが許され、港は 19 世紀まで繁栄しました。現在では、ビクトリア時代の港湾施設が再開発され、当時の倉庫は、博物館、レストラン、オフィスとして活気にあふれています。

Painswick

ATTRACTIONS, EVENTS, AND POINTS OF INTEREST

- Fossil Exhibition, at the Shetland Shop – Open all year – . Fine displays of rocks, minerals and fossils, including a live coral reef.
- Gloucestershire Guild of Craftsmen – Open all year Tuesday to Saturday – 01242 245215. The Gallery displays and sells crafts made by Guild members. An annual exhibition is held throughout August in the Painswick Centre.
- Painswick Rococo Garden – January to November – 01452 813204.

18th century garden with maze, children's trail, licensed restaurant and gift shop. Breathtaking carpets of snowdrops in winter/early spring.
- Wonders from the Earth – Open all year – . An exhibition of natural rarities.
- Painswick Beacon affords magnificent views across The Severn Valley and the Welsh mountains. There is also an 18-hole golf course.
- St Mary's churchyard has 99 yew trees. Legend states the 100th will not grow.
- The stocks are unusually made of iron.
- A Victorian Market Day is held in July.

The pale grey stone of the western Cotswolds gives Painswick a different feel to many of the honey coloured Cotswold stone settlements. The town prospered in the 17th and 18th centuries when the fast flowing streams powered cloth mills and created prosperity for the owners, who built fine houses in the town from stone quarried at nearby Painswick Beacon.

Set among the woodland of the steep western slopes near the escarpment, Painswick is an ideal base for exploring on foot, with fabulous views back to the town or glimpses of the incised countryside and sheltered villages such as Slad (made famous by Laurie Lee in *Cider with Rosie*). Among the many delightful walks in the area is the Cotswold Way, Painswick is about midway along this 100 mile route.

There are rare 17th century spectacle stocks near the court house. 14th century houses in Bisley Street include two original Donkey doors, Wide enough for panniered donkeys who carried the wool from the mills along the local valleys.

La pierre gris pale de l'ouest des Cotswolds donne à Painswick une atmosphère différente de celle des autres villages des Cotswolds à la pierre plus dorée. Située en hauteur au-dessus de pentes abruptes, la ville s'épanouit au 17ème et 18ème siècles lorsque les torrents faisaient fonctionner les filatures et enrichissaient leurs propriétaires, qui construisirent de belles demeures en ville en pierre extraite des carrières voisines de Painswick Beacon.

Etablie au milieu des bois sur les pentes accentuées de l'ouest, près de l'escarpement, Painswick est une base de promenade idéale, avec des points de vue fabuleux sur la ville, la campagne et les villages abrités rendu fameux par l'écrivain Laurie Lee.

L'église St Mary essentiellement du 15ème et 16ème siècle est surtout connue pour son cimetière dans lequel 99 ifs poussent entre des pierres tombales aux sculptures très travaillées.

Der blassgraue Stein der westlichen Cotswolds gibt Painswick einen anderen Ausdruck als die mehr honigfarbenen Cotswold-Siedlungen. Über steilen Hängen gelegen, prosperierte die Stadt im 17. und 18. Jahrhundert als die schnell-fließenden Bäche zum Antrieb von Webereien genutzt wurden und Wohlstand für deren Eigentümer brachte, die sich in der Stadt prächtige Häuser aus dem am nahegelegenen Painswick Beacon gehauenen Stein bauten.

Inmitten der Waldlandschaft der steilen westlichen Hänge nahe der Kante der Cotswolds gelegen, ist Painswick ein idealer Ausgangspunkt für Wanderungen mit sagenhaften Aussichten auf die Stadt, Landschaft und geschützt liegenden Dörfer, die durch Laurie Lee berühmt wurden.

St. Mary's Church, größtenteils aus dem 15. und 16. Jahrhundert, ist am besten bekannt für ihren Kirchhof, wo 99 gestutzte Eiben zwischen kompliziert behauenen Grabsteinen paradieren.

ペインズウィックのコッツウォルズ西部の灰白色の石を使った家並みは、クリーム色の石を見慣れた目には新鮮に映ります。急峻な崖の上に建つこの町は、17〜18 世紀にかけて、急流を利用した毛織物工業で繁栄し、経営者たちはその富によって、近くのペインズウィック ビーコン（Painswick Beacon）の採石場から切り出した石を使い、壮麗な家を建てました。

ペインズウィックは、コッツウォルズ丘陵西端の森林地帯にあり、ここを起点にあたりを散策すれば、すばらしい景観を楽しみ、作家ローリー・リーによって紹介された牧歌的な村の生活を垣間見ることができます。

15〜16 世紀に建てられたこの町のセント マリー教会は、見事な 99 本のイチイの木と華麗な彫刻を施した墓石のある庭で有名です。

Stroud

Located at the convergence of five deep river valleys, Stroud made a natural industrial centre for the Cotswolds. This is an area rich both in verdant undulating landscape and industrial heritage of waterwheels and looms. At its peak in the 18th and early 19th centuries 150 fulling mills worked in the Chalford valley, the fast-flowing soft water vital in the production of high quality cloth. Stroudwater scarlet and Uley blues were in great demand for military uniforms. Of the 30 mills still standing today only one produces cloth.

The town's streets are spread over steep slopes and its centre focuses at the 19th century Subscription rooms. There are many interesting shops and cafes and the town has built up a reputation for addressing a wide range of environmental issues.

ATTRACTIONS, EVENTS, AND POINTS OF INTEREST

- Market Days - Friday and Saturday. Farmers' Market - every Saturday.
- The Museum in the Park – Open all year – 01453 763394. Situated in Stratford Park, this family-friendly museum opened in December 2000 and features the world's first lawnmower and a Laurie Lee exhibition (free).
- The Subscription Rooms – Open all year – Houses the Tourist centre. Its forecourt will be the focus of a range of outdoor events throughout the year.
- An annual Art Festival is held each April/May.
- Britain's last duel was fought here in 1807. The loser, Lieutenant Delmont, is buried in St Laurence churchyard.
- Centre of 5 valleys. Many trails to explore and magnificent views surround Stroud.
- Medieval Hall, High Street. The oldest building discovered in Stroud has been carefully restored.
- The name Stroud derives from an old English word, Stród, meaning 'marshy ground overgrown with brushwood'.
- Arts Centre - Events and exhibitions held throughout the year.

Stonehouse

Installée au confluent de cinq vallées profondes, Stroud fut naturellement un centre industriel pour les Cotswolds ; c'est une region riche par ses paysages vallonnes et par son heritage industriel de moulins à eau et de tissages. Au sommet de sa puissance au 18ème et au début du 19ème siècle, on comptait 150 filatures dans la vallée de Chalford dont l'eau douce et vive était vitale pour la production de toile de bonne qualité. Le rouge « Stroudwater » et les bleus « Uley » étaient très demandés pour fabriquer les uniformes militaires. Des 30 filatures qui existent encore de nos jours une seule fabrique de la toile.

Il y a beaucoup de magasins et de cafés intéressants et la ville a la réputation de bien maîtriser toutes les questions relatives à l'environnement.

Am Zusammenfluss von fünf tiefen Flusstälern gelegen, ist Stroud ein natürliches industrielles Zentrum für die Cotswolds, einem Gebiet das sowohl reich an grüner hügeliger Landschaft als auch an industriellem Erbe an Wasserrädern und Webstühlen ist. Auf seinem Höhepunkt im 18. und zeitigen 19. Jahrhundert arbeiteten 150 Webereien im Chalford-Tal, dessen schnell-fließendes weiches Wasser äußerst wichtig für die Herstellung hochwertigen Tuches war. Stroudwater-Rot und Uley-Blau waren sehr gefragt für militärische Uniformen. Von den 30 Webereien die heute noch in Betrieb sind, produziert nur noch eine Tuch.

Es gibt viele interessante Geschäfte und verstreute Cafés. Die Stadt hat einen guten Ruf für das Ansprechen einer Vielzahl von Umweltfragen erworben.

5 本の川が集まる緑濃い谷間にあるストラウドは、水車を利用した機織りによって、コッツウォルズの産業の中心地になっていました。流速の速い軟水が高品質の毛織物の生産に適していたため、18世紀から19世紀初期のこの町の最盛期には、150もの縮充工場がチャルフォード（Chalford）の谷で操業していました。ストラウドウォーター（Stroudwater）の緋色とユーレイ（Uley）の青色のビロードは軍服には欠かすことができません。現在も稼動している30の水車のうち、紡織に利用されているのは1つだけです。

ストラウドには、興味深い店や喫茶店がたくさんあります。また、環境問題に真剣に取り組んでいる町としても知られています。

Area 2 General

OTHER ATTRACTIONS IN AREA 2

Cattle Country Adventure Park, Berkeley – Open all year – 01453 810510. Unusual breeds including bison and wild boar. Adventure playgrounds for children and adults. Restaurant and function room.

Cheese Rolling, Coopers Hill near Cheltenham. A bizarre event held each Spring Bank Holiday. Local people of all ages chase rounds of cheese down the very steep Coopers Hill.

Coaley Peak, between Stroud and Dursley. Spectacular views west over the river Severn and an ancient burial chamber, the Nympsfield Long Barrow.

Crickley Hill Country Park, Birdlip – Open all year – 01452 863170. 144 acres of limestone grassland and beech woodland on the Cotswold Scarp with views towards Gloucester, way marked trails and Visitor Centre.

Frampton Court, Frampton-on-Severn – Limited opening – 01452 740267. Grade 1 listed building and fine example of a Georgian Stately Home.

Misarden Park Gardens, Miserden – Limited opening April to September – 01285 821303. Fine gardens dating from 1620.

The National Birds of Prey Centre. Newent. One of the world's largest collections of birds of prey. Flying demonstrations daily. Café, tearoom and shop - 01531 820286.

Nature in Art, Wallsworth Hall, Twigworth – Open all year – 01452 731422. The world's first museum dedicated to art inspired by nature.

Prinknash Abbey Park, Cranham – Open all year – 01452 812455. A modern Abbey with visitors centre, tearooms and gift shop, bird and animal park.

Three Choirs Vineyard, Newent – Open all year – 01531 890223. One of the best-known English vineyards. Restaurant and regular tastings.

Woodchester Mansion, Nympsfield – Limited opening – 01453 861541. An unfinished Victorian masterpiece set in a secluded valley south of Stroud with a most interesting history.

Woodchester Mansion

OTHER PLACES OF INTEREST IN AREA 2

The old market town of Newent lies north west of Gloucester, home of the National Birds of Prey Centre, and the Three Choirs Vineyard. Wales is less than 20 miles away, either through Ross-On-Wye, or south through The Forest of Dean. Along the river Severn small villages, many with public houses, are ideal locations for lunch, or a base for river walks.

Overlooking Gloucester to the east is Birdlip and Crickley Hill Park, a National Trust site and part of an Iron Age promontory fort. South towards Stroud, the villages of Sheepscombe, Whiteway, Slad, Bisley and Miserden shelter in a deep wooded valley. It is well worth exploring the minor roads as they often afford spectacular views. The valley is one of the five which lead to Stroud, each with it's own character. Old woollen mills, most restored for modern use, are still evident. Other National Trust sites, Minchinhampton and Rodborough Commons have views across Stroud, Nailsworth and the river Severn. These are ideal picnic sites with public houses and a golf course. To the west on the road to Frampton on Severn, Stonehouse is a good base to explore the Stroudwater Canal.

Bisley

Autres Lieux Intéressants : Région 2
   Au nord ouest de Gloucester s'étend la vieille ville commerçante de Newent, siège du Centre National des Oiseaux de Proie, ainsi que le vignoble "Three Choirs Vineyard". Le pays de Galles est à moins de 20 miles. A l'est Birdlip et Crickley Hill Park, qui appartient au National Trust et les restes d'un promontoire fortifié de l'age du fer surplombent Gloucester et au sud vers Stroud les villages de Sheepscombe, Whiteway, Slad, Bisley et Miserden s'abritent dans de profondes vallées boisées.
   On peut encore voir de vieilles filatures de laine dans les cinq vallées de Stroud, certaines ont été restaurées. Les sites du National Trust à Minchinhampton et Rodborough Commons permettent des vues superbes sur Stroud, Nailsworth et la Severn et sont aussi des lieux de pique-nique parfaits. A l'ouest vers Frampton-on-Severn se trouve Stonehouse une excellente base de départ pour une promenade idyllique le long du canal de Stroudwater.

Weitere Sehenswerte Orte – Gebiet 2
   Nordwestlich von Gloucester liegt das alte Marktstädtchen Newent, die Heimat des Nationalen Raubvogelzentrums und des Three Choirs Weinberges. Wales ist weniger als 30 km entfernt. Nach Osten hin überblicken Birdlip und der Crickley Hill Park, ein Gelände des National Trust und Teil eines Forts aus der Eisenzeit, Gloucester und nach Süden hin verstecken sich Stroud, Sheepscombe, Whiteway, Slad, Bisley und Miserden in tiefen bewaldeten Tälern.
   Alte Wollwebereien, die für die moderne Nutzung wiederhergestellt wurden, sind noch in Strouds fünf Tälern zu sehen. Das National Trust Gelände in Minchinhampton und Rodborough Commons bieten schöne Aussichten auf Stroud, Nailsworth und den Fluss Severn und sind ideale Picknickplätze. Westlich, in Richtung Frampton-on-Severn liegt Stonehouse, ein guter Ausgangspunkt für einen idyllischen Spaziergang am Stroudwater Canal entlang.

その他の見どころ ― エリア 2
   グロスターの北西にある古くからの市場町、ニューウェント（Newent）には、猛禽類センター（National Birds of Prey Centre）とブドウ園（Three Choirs Vineyard）があります。ここからウェールズまではおよそ30キロです。グロスターの東のバードリップ（Birdlip）とクリックリー ヒル公園（Crickley Hill Park）には、見晴らしのよい崖の上にナショナル トラストが管理する鉄器時代の砦跡があります。ここと南のストラウドとの間には、シープスコム（Sheepscombe）、ホワイトウェイ（Whiteway）、スラッド（Slad）、ビズリー（Bisley）、ミザーデン（Miserden）などの村々が緑の谷間の奥にひっそりとしたたたずまいを見せています。
   ストラウドの５つの谷間にあった毛織物工場は、用途は変わりましたが、現在でも残っています。ナショナル トラストが管理するミンシンハンプトン コモン（Minchinhampton Common）とロドバラー コモン（Rodborough Common）は、ストラウド、ネイルズワース、セバーン川を見渡せるピクニックに最適の場所です。ストラウドの西にあるフランプトン オン セバーン（Frampton-on-Severn）にはりっぱな石造りの建物が残っているほか、ここを起点にストラウドウォーター運河に沿って田園風景の中をのんびりと散策することができます。

Winchcombe

One of the Cotswolds earliest tourist destinations, Winchcombe was a place of pilgrimage during medieval times when the faithful flocked to visit the tomb of the martyred Kenelm, son of the Saxon King Kenulf. The abbey became wealthy but following dissolution only one wall and the abbey church remained. The 15th century Church of St Peter's still harbours a stone coffin rumoured to be that of Kenelm.

The names Vineyard Street and Tobacco Close record some of the more unusual crops grown on the steep slopes that surround Winchcombe. Winchcombe is a place worthy of exploration; its streets reveal a great variety of character, with timber-framed buildings cheek by jowl with more substantial stone houses. Interesting shops, traditional teashops, good pubs and a local pottery are among its attractions.

- TIC Town Hall, High Street, Winchcombe, 01242 602925 (Restricted service during the winter - Saturday and Sunday's).
- TIC The Wilson, Cheltenham Art Gallery and Museum. 01242 387488.

ATTRACTIONS, EVENTS, AND POINTS OF INTEREST

- Hailes Abbey – Open April to October – 01242 602398. The ruins of this 13th century Cistercian Abbey now include a fascinating museum. Special events are held here during the summer. An English Heritage site.
- Sudeley Castle - gardens only open – Open March to October - 01242 604244.
- Winchcombe Folk and Police Museum – Open April to October – 07922 081742 (during opening hours only). History of the town from Neolithic times and collection of police uniforms.
- Winchcombe Pottery – Open all year – 01242 602462. Possibly the longest running pottery in the country.

Hailes Abbey

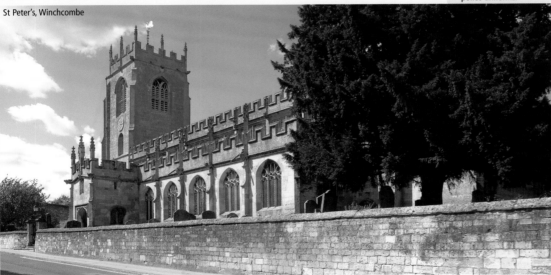

St Peter's, Winchcombe

Probablement l'une des toutes premières destinations touristiques des Cotswolds, Winchcombe était un lieu de pèlerinage au moyen-age pour les croyants qui venaient nombreux se recueillir sur la tombe du martyr Kenelm, fils du roi saxon Kenulf. L'église St Peter's du 15ème siècle abrite encore un sarcophage dont la rumeur dit qu'il serait celui de Kenelm.

Les noms Vineyard Street (rue du Vignoble) et Tobacco Close (impasse du Tabac) témoignent de certaines cultures plus surprenantes établies, à la suite du déclin du commerce de la laine, sur les coteaux escarpés qui entourent Winchcombe. Winchcombe est une ville qu'il faut découvrir à pied ; ses rues recèlent une grande variété de styles, avec des maisons à colombages cotoyant des maisons plus cossues en pierre. Des salons de thé traditionnels, des magasins intéressants et un atelier de poterie local contribuent aussi à l'intérêt de la ville.

Winchcombe war möglicherweise eines der ersten touristischen Ziele in den Cotswolds. Während des Mittelalters war es ein Wallfahrtsort für die Gläubigen, die in Scharen herbeikamen um das Grab des Märtyrers Kenelm, dem Sohn des Sachsenkönigs Kenulf, zu besuchen. Die St Peter's Kirche aus dem Is. Jahrhundert beherbergt noch einen steinernen Sarg der angelolich der von Kenelm sein soll.

Die Namen Vineyard Street und Tobacco Close zeugen von einigen eher ungewöhnlichen Pflanzen, die nach dem Rückgang des Wollhandels an den steilen Hängen um Winchcombe angebaut wurden. Winchcombe ist ein erkundenswerter Ort; seine Straßen zeigen eine große Gestaltungsvielfalt mit Fachwerkhäusern Seite an Seite mit soliden Steinhäusern. Besondere Attraktionen sind seine traditionellen Teestuben, interessante Geschäfte und eine örtliche Töpferei.

中世の頃から巡礼の歴訪地だったウィンチコムは、コッツウォルズで最も古い観光地といってもよいでしょう。当時の信者たちは、サクソン王ケヌルフ（Kenulf）の息子、殉教者ケネルム（Kenelm）の墓に詣でるためにここを訪れました。15 世紀に建築されたセント ピーター教会には、ケネルムのものといわれる石棺が今に残ります。

「ぶどう園通り」（Vineyard Street）、「たばこ小路」（Tobacco Close）といった名前から、毛織物工業の衰退後、英国では珍しい農産物がこの町の周囲の丘で栽培されていたことがわかります。古い木骨構造の家やどっしりとした石造りの家が肩を寄せ合うウィンチコムの通りを散策すると、思いがけないこの町の歴史に出会うことができます。散策に疲れたら英国伝統の喫茶店で一休み、地元の店や陶器製作所なども訪れてみたいものです。

Cheltenham

A small market town in the early 18th century, Cheltenham had become a regency town of wide streets and elegant proportions by the mid-19th century, built around the fame of its healing alkaline water. In 1788 King George III gave the water his royal approval and in 1816 the Duke of Wellington was apparently cured of a liver disorder; Cheltenham was established as a centre for rich seekers of good health.

The town has some of Britain's finest regency architecture, including Pittville Pump Room, the Promenade, the Queen's Hotel and the Rotunda, all restored in the early 20th century.

As well as many international festivals Cheltenham is the home of National Hunt racing, the highlight of which is the Gold Cup in March. The town attracts many shoppers, drawn not only by the range of shops but also the wide avenues and floral displays. The variety of wine-bars, restaurants, pubs and clubs make Cheltenham ideal for a great night out.

■ **TIC The Wilson, Cheltenham Art Gallery and Museum.. 01242 387488**

ATTRACTIONS, EVENTS, AND POINTS OF INTEREST
■ Market Day - Thursday.
  Farmers' Market - 2nd & last Friday.
■ Cheltenham Art Gallery and Museum – Open all year – 01242 387488. Collection of furniture and silverware, café and shop. The Edward Wilson Gallery chronicles the life of the Cheltenham born Antarctic explorer.
■ Cheltenham Racecourse. – 01242 513014. Home of National Hunt racing, host to the famous Cheltenham Gold Cup and 15 other fixtures between October and May.
■ The Cheltenham Hall of Fame – Open all year – 01242 513014. At the Racecourse complex, it charts the history of steeple chasing from 1819.
■ The Everyman Theatre – Box Office 01242 572573.
■ Holst Birthplace Museum – 01242 524846. A regency terrace house where the composer was born in 1874. Working kitchen and Holst's original piano.
■ Pittville Pump Room – Open all year (10am-4pm. Closed Tuesdays) – 01242 387409. An imaginative exhibition of

costume from Regency times to the Sixties. The famous Spa waters are still there to taste from the original pump. The grounds include children's play area, pet corner and boating lake.
■ Cheltenham Festivals Box office (All) 01242 850270
■ Cheltenham Cricket Festival. Held each summer at Cheltenham College in honour of W.G.Grace, it is the oldest cricket festival in the country.
■ The Cheltenham Festival of Literature in October is the largest of its kind in the country and attracts top names from journalism, broadcasting, television and the stage.
■ The Cheltenham Folk Festival is held each February.
■ The International Festival of Music, held every July, focuses on contemporary orchestral and chamber classical music.
■ The International Jazz Festival is now a permanent fixture on the international jazz calendar and held each April.
■ The elegant Town Hall hosts major festivals, classical and contemporary music, comedy and much more. 0844 576 2210 Charges apply.

Petite bourgade commerçante au début du 18ème siècle, Cheltenham s'était transformée en une nouvelle ville Régence avant le milieu du 19ème siècle, bâtie autour de la réputation de ses eaux thermales aux vertus curatives. En 1788 le roi George III donna son agrément royal aux eaux thermales et en 1816 le duc de Wellington fut apparemment guéri de troubles du foie.
  La ville possède des exemples d'architecture Régence parmi les plus raffinés de Grande Bretagne, dont la Pittville Pump Room, où l'on peut encore goûter les eaux, la Promenade, le Queen's Hôtel et la Rotunde.
  C'est la capitale des courses hippiques du National Hunt, dont l'apothéose est la Gold Cup en mars. Le shopping est une des grandes attractions de la ville qui séduit non seulement par ses nombreux magasins mais aussi par ses larges avenues et sa décoration florale.

War Cheltenham im frühen 18. Jahrhundert nur ein kleiner Marktflecken, so hatte es sich bis zur Mitte des 19. Jahrhunderts zu einer neuen Regentschaftsstadt entwickelt, erbaut auf dem Ruhm seines heilenden alkalischen Wassers. Im Jahre 1788 erhielt das Wasser von König George III seine königliche Anerkennung, und im Jahre 1816 wurde der Duke von Wellington hier angeblich von einer Leberkrankheit geheilt.
  Die Stadt besitzt eine der schönsten Regentschafts-Architekturen in ganz Großbritannien; dazu zählen die Pittville Trinkhalle, wo man nach wie vor das Heilwasser probieren kann, die Promenade, das Queen's Hotel und die Rotunde.
  Cheltenham ist die Heimat des National Hunt Pferderennens, dessen Höhepunkt der Gold Cup im März ist. Die Stadt ist eine Attraktion für viele Kauflustige, die nicht nur von der Vielfalt der Geschäfte sondern auch von den breiten Boulevards und Blumenanlagen angezogen werden.

18 世紀に小さな市場町として始まったチェルトナムは、健康増進を増進するアルカリ性鉱泉が 1788 年にジョージ 3 世国王による勅許を得たことや 1816 年にウェリントン公爵の肝臓疾患がこの鉱 泉によって治癒したことなどで有名になり、19 世紀の中頃には、この鉱泉を中心として摂政時代様 式の新しい町として変貌を遂げました。
  現在のチェルトナムは、英国で最も豪華な摂政時代様式の建築で知られ、今でも鉱水を試飲でき るピットビル (Pittville) ポンプ室や、プロムナード (Promenade)、クイーンズ ホテル (Queen's Hotel)、円形建築物ロタンダ (Rotunda) などが有名です。
  チェルトナムは毎年 3 月に開催されるゴールド カップ レースで有名なナショナル ハント競馬の 開催地としても知られているほか、ショッピング センターや花のあふれる広い街路は多くの買い物 客でにぎわっています。

Northleach

- VIC in the Corinium Museum, Park Street, Cirencester, Gloucestershire, GL7 2BX. 01285 655611/654180

ATTRACTIONS, EVENTS, AND POINTS OF INTEREST

- Market Day - Wednesday.
- The World of Mechanical Music – Open all year – 01451 860181. An award winning museum of antique clocks, musical boxes, mechanical musical instruments that are maintained in perfect order and are introduced and played by the guides in the form of live entertainment. Enchanting shop.
- The Church of St Peter and St Paul display some of the finest wool merchant brasses in the country.
- There are many lovely areas around Northleach for exploring and walking, please keep dogs under control as many fields have livestock

Dominating this small town is one of the finest 'wool' churches in the Cotswolds, the 15th century church of St Peter and St Paul with its 30 metre tower. A fine example of perpendicular style, the church was built with the funds of wealthy medieval wool merchants who prospered in what was one of the most important wool towns in the centre of a large sheep-rearing area.

Close to the Fosse Way and on the London to Gloucester route, Northleach became a stopping point during the age of coach travel; the old road has now been replaced by a by-pass, to the benefit of the town's people and historic properties.

Just to the west of the town the 18th century 'House of Correction' now houses the Cotswold Conservation Board.

L'église qui domine cette petite ville est l'une des plus belles églises 'de la laine' des Cotswolds. Cette église du 15ème siècle, St Peter and St Paul, fut érigée grâce aux dons de riches négociants en laine du moyen-age qui prospérèrent dans ce qui était l'une des plus importantes villes lainières de la région. L'église abrite certains des plus beaux bronzes monumentaux des Cotswolds.

Située à proximité de la Fosse Way et sur la route de Londres à Gloucester, Northleach devint une étape à la période des voyages en car; la route contourne désormais la ville, pour le plus grand profit des habitants et des monuments historiques. A l'ouest de la ville la Maison d'Arrêt du 18ème siècle est maintenant occupée par le musée de la vie rurale traditionnelle des Cotswolds.

Dieses Städtchen wird dominiert von einer der schönsten „Wollkirchen" in den Cotswolds. St. Peter und Paul wurde im 15. Jahrhundert mit den Geldern wohlhabender Wollhändler gebaut, die in dieser, einer der bedeutsamsten Wollstädte der Gegend, prosperierten. Die Kirche beherrbergt noch immer einige der schönsten Messinggrabplatten in den Cotswolds.

An der Strecke von London nach Gloucester und nahe dem Fosse Way gelegen, entwickelte sich Northleach im Zeitalter der Kutschreisen zu einem Rastplatz. Sehr zum Nutzen der Bewohner und der historischen Gebäude der Stadt wurde die alte Straße mittlerweile durch eine Umgehungsstraße ersetzt. Westlich der Stadt befindet sich die „Besserungsanstalt" aus dem 18. Jahrhundert, die heute ein Museum über das traditionelle ländliche Leben in den Cotswolds beherbergt.

ノースリーチの「セント ピーターおよびセント ポール教会」（Church of St Peter and St Paul）は、中世の富裕なコッツウォルズの羊毛商人によって建てられた数ある教会の中でも最も優れたものといわれています。15 世紀に建てられたこの教会に残る美しい黄銅製の記念碑を見ると、この小さな町が当時は羊毛産業の中心地として繁栄していたことがわかります。

住民の希望により、駅馬車時代のフォッス街道と、ロンドンとグロスターをつなぐ街道に代わってバイパスが建設されたので、歴史的な建物が旧道沿いに今も残っています。ノースリーチの西側にある 18 世紀の教護院は、現在は博物館としてコッツウォルズの伝統的な農村の生活を今に伝えています。

Area 3 General

OTHER ATTRACTIONS IN AREA 3

Chedworth Roman Villa, Chedworth – Open March to November – 01242 890256. Dating from 120AD, now a National Trust site, it is one of the finest preserved Roman settlements in the country. Events held throughout the year.

Gloucestershire and Warwickshire Steam Railway, Toddington – Open March to December – 01242 621405. Trips with views of the Cotswolds and Malverns.

John Moore Countryside Museum, Tewkesbury – Open April to October – 01684 297174. Displays of British woodland and wetland life.

Lodge Park, Aldsworth – Open March to November – 01451 844130. 17th century deer coursing park, with a restored grandstand dating from 1634. The estate car parks and footpaths are open all year.

Sherborne Park Estate, Sherborne – A National Trust site encompassing the village, water meadows, a pleasure ground and 3 deer parks. An abundance of wildlife may be seen from the marked footpaths although they are not rights of way and may be closed at various times.

Stanway House, Stanway – Limited opening – 01386 584469. A Jacobean manor house with an impressive gatehouse and beautiful gardens, with Britain's largest fountain (over 300ft high).

Tewkesbury Abbey, Tewkesbury – Open all year – 01684 850959. Approximately 900 years old, it was the last abbey to be dissolved by Henry VIII. There are daily guided tours and gift shop.

OTHER PLACES OF INTEREST IN AREA 3

Tewkesbury lies at the confluence of the rivers Severn and Avon approximately 10 miles north of Cheltenham. The imposing Abbey overlooks historic black and white houses and inns. To the east the Cotswold escarpment climbs to it's highest point at Cleeve Cloud, on Cleeve Common, a municipal golf course with views of the Malverns and the Black Mountains in Wales.

South of Winchcombe, one of the most unexplored and picturesque valleys in the Cotswolds leads past Humblebee Wood to Charlton Abbots, Brockhampton and Sevenhampton, eventually reaching the A40 at Andoversford. Further south through more wooded valleys lie Withington and Chedworth.

Another charming route runs parallel to the north of the A40 from Northleach to Burford. It follows the river Sherborne from its source near Farmington, through the village of Sherborne to the river Windrush.

Stanway House

Tewkesbury Abbey

OTHER TICs
- Tewkesbury Visitor and Heritage Centre,100 Church Street, GL20 5AB 01684 855040
- TIC 4 High Street, Upton-upon-Severn. 01684 594200.
- TIC Malvern, Lyttelton Well Courtyard, 6 Church Street, WR14 2AY 01684 892289.

Autres Lieux Intéressants : Région 3
A 16 km au nord de Cheltenham, la ville historique de Tewkesbury est établie au confluent de la Severn et de l'Avon, avec son imposante abbaye qui surplombe les maisons et les auberges noires et blanches. C'est entre Winchcombe et Cheltenham, au centre de Cleeve Common, que se trouve le sommet de l'escarpement des Cotswolds, qui offre une vue à couper le souffle sur les Malverns et plus loin sur les montagnes galloises. Plus au sud le long de la crête de l'escarpement, sur le «Cotswolds Way», on peut voir un relief calcaire impressionnant connu dans la région sous le nom de Devil's Chimney (la cheminée du diable).
Au sud de Winchcombe on trouve l'une des vallées les plus pittoresques et les moins visitées des Cotswolds. Elle mène à Charlton Abbots, Brockhamton et Sevenhampton en passant par Humblebee Wood, et atteint finalement la A40 à Andoversford. Plus au sud, après des vallées plus boisées, on trouve Withington et Chedworth.

Weitere Sehenswerte Orte – Gebiet 3
Am Zusammenfluss der Flüsse Severn und Avon, 16 km nördlich von Cheltenham, liegt die historische Stadt Tewkesbury von deren beeindruckender Abtei aus man die historischen schwarz-weißen Häuser und Gasthöfe überblicken kann. Zwischen Winchcombe und Cheltenham, im Zentrum von Cleeve Common, erreichen die Cotswolds ihren höchsten Punkt und bieten eine überwältigende Aussicht auf die Malverns und darüber hinaus bis zu den Waliser Bergen. Südlich, entlang der Kante der Erhebung, am Cotswold Way, befindet sich eine gigantische Felsnase aus Kalkstein die örtlich als Kamin des Teufels bekannt ist.
Südlich von Winchcombe liegt eines der unberührtesten und malerischsten Täler der Cotswolds. Es führt am Humblebee Wood vorbei nach Charlton Abbots, Brockhampton und Sevenhampton, bevor es letztlich bei Andoversford die Landstraße A40 erreicht. Weiter südlich, durch mehr bewaldete Täler, liegen Withington und Chedworth.

その他の見どころ ― エリア 3
チェルトナムの北、約16キロのところにあるテュークスベリー（Tewkesbury）は、セバーン川とエーボン川の合流点です。白と黒に塗られた古い木骨構造の家並みを見下ろすように修道院が建っています。ウィンチコムとチェルトナムの中間にあるクリーブ コモン（Cleeve Common）の中心がコッツウォルド丘陵の最高地点です。ここからの眺望はすばらしく、晴れた日には遠くウェールズの山々を背景にモルバーンの丘や美しい英国の田園風景が楽しめます。コッツウォルド街道が通る丘陵の南端では、地元で「悪魔の煙突」（Devil's Cimney）と呼ぶ突出した石灰岩の地形が見られます。
ウィンチコムの南のひなびた谷間にはハンブルビーの森（Humblebee Wood）が広がり、チャールトン アボッツ（Charlton Abbots）、ブロックハンプトン（Brockhampton）、セブンハンプトン（Sevenhampton）の村々を通ってアンドーバーズフォード（Andoversford）でA40号線に接続しています。さらに南に広がる谷間の森の中にはウィジントン（Withington）とチェドワース（Chedworth）の村があります。

Stow-on-the-Wold

The highest Cotswold town sits at the hub of eight roads, including the Fosse Way. An ideal location for a market, by 1107 it was renowned for its two annual charter fairs. Stow was an important centre for the wool trade until the decline in sheep farming when it turned its attention to horses. Annual horse fairs are still held in May and October, but Stow's greatest trade is now in antiques and crafts, and the many shops in the towns old stone buildings help to make this a popular place with visitors.

The large market square remains at the heart of the town, such a space is untypical of Cotswold towns. The original market cross was renovated by townspeople in 1878, thanking the Lord of the Manor for providing a deep well, so that water no longer had to be carried up the hill. The market square is surrounded by 17th and 18th century buildings, many of which house attractive pubs and coaching inns, which continue to refresh the weary traveller.

■ **VIC St Edwards Hall, The Square, Stow On The Wold, GL54 1AF. 01451 870998**

ATTRACTIONS, EVENTS, AND POINTS OF INTEREST

- ■ The last important battle of the English Civil War ended in the square in 1646.
- ■ A contemporary of Rubens and Van Dyck, Gaspar de Craeyer was responsible for the painting of The Crucifixion in the south aisle of St Edward's church.
- ■ The Kings Arms in the Square is a classic example of an old coaching inn where the main entrance leads through an arch to the stables. Charles 1 stayed here at the time of the battle of Naseby.
- ■ The Royalist Hotel in Digbeth Street is said to be the oldest inn in England.
- ■ The Stocks, although replaced, have existed on the green in The Square since the 15th century.
- ■ Farmers' Market - 2nd Thursday of each month 9am - 1.30pm.

La ville la plus haute des Cotswolds est établie au carrefour de huit routes y compris la Fosse Way. Situation idéale pour une ville commerçante, elle était déjà renomme en 1107 pour ses deux foires annuelles. Stow resta longtemps un des centres du négoce des ovins jusqu'au déclin de l'élevage des moutons et se tourna alors vers celui des chevaux. Une foire aux chevaux se tient encore tous les ans en mai, mais le commerce le plus important à Stow est aujourd'hui celui des antiquités et de l'artisanat.

La large place du marché, espace urbain atypique dans les cotswolds, existe encore, et est entourée de jolis bâtiments des 17ème et 18ème siècles. La croix originale de la place du marché fut restaurée par les habitants en 1878 en remerciement au Lord local qui avait fait creuser un puits très profond afin que l'on ait plus à aller chercher l'eau en bas de la colline.

Die höchstgelegenste Stadt der Cotswolds liegt an der Kreuzung von acht Straßen, einschließlich dem Fosse Way. Als idealer Marktstandort, war es schon um 1107 berühmt für seine zwei jährlichen Chartermärkte. Stow blieb ein bedeutendes Zentrum des Schafhandels bis zum Rückgang der Schafzucht, als es sein Interesse den Pferden zuwandte. Alljährlich im Mai findet ein Pferdemarkt statt, aber Stow's größter Handel besteht heutzutage in Antiquitäten und im Kunsthandwerk.

Der für Cotswoldstädte untypische, große Marktplatz ist noch erhalten und umgeben von prächtigen Gebäuden aus dem 17. und 18. Jahrhundert. Das ursprüngliche Marktkreuz wurde 1878 von Bürgern der Stadt renoviert, als Dank an den Gutsherren für die Bereitstellung eines tiefen Brunnens, so dass das Wasser nicht mehr den Berg hinauf getragen werden musste.

ストウ オン ザ ウォルドは、コッツウォルズで最も標高の高い町です。フォッス街道を含む 8 本の道路がここに集まっており、市場として理想的な立地条件を備えています。1107 年には、すでに年に 2 回開催される定期市で有名でした。この町は、長い間重要な羊の集散地でしたが、その後、牧羊が下火となり、馬を中心とした牧畜へと変わっていきました。現在でも、毎年 5 月には馬市が開かれます。しかし、現在のストウ オン ザ ウォルドの商業は骨董品と工芸品が中心です。

コッツウォルズの町には珍しく、市場開催のための大きな広場があります。この 17〜18 世紀の美しい建物に囲まれた広場には、1878 年に、荘園領主が深井戸を掘り、これ以降水汲みの重労働から解放されたことを感謝する住民によって改築された市場十字が建っています。

Upper and Lower Slaughter

Stone and slate from local quarries was extensively used in these villages, its quality was such that some went further afield, including to Oxford (in the 1450s) for parts of New College roof.

Unspoilt cottages built in traditional Cotswold style border the river Eye in Lower Slaughter, the banks linked by a series of low stone bridges. Beside the church the Manor House, built by Cotswold Master Mason Valentine Strong in about 1650, is now an hotel. The 19th century corn mill with its brick chimney seems a little out of place, but the original water mill may have pre-dated the Domesday book.

Half a mile upstream, Upper Slaughter's Tudor manor has been described as one of the most beautiful in the Cotswolds, embodying many of the features of local architecture in its mellow stonework. More pastoral than its neighbour, the cottages and farms of Upper Slaughter cluster near the forded river Eye.

These villages blend agelessly into the landscape; the visitor who takes time to walk around them, or along the riverside path joining the two communities, perhaps best appreciates their atmosphere.

- VIC VIC St Edwards Hall, The Square, Stow On The Wold, GL54 1AF. 01451 870998
- VIC Victoria Street, Bourton-on-the-Water. 01451 820211

ATTRACTIONS, EVENTS, AND POINTS OF INTEREST
- Old Mill Museum – Open all year (January and February weekends only) – 01451 820052. Restored mill, tearooms and gift shop.
- The church of St Peter contains a monument to F.E. Witts, 19th century rector and Lord of the Manor who wrote 'Diary of a Cotswold Parson.'
- The Slaughters name derives from an Anglo-Saxon word *slohtre* meaning 'muddy place'.
- Apart from renovation work no new houses have been built in Upper Slaughter since 1904.
- The village hall holds exhibitions from April throughout the summer months of work from local artists, including Lesley Holmes who, apart from her local work, is probably best known for her illustrations of the James Herriot books.

Upper Slaughter

Lower Slaughter

Dès 1452 des ardoises provenant de carrières locales sont acheminées vers Oxford pour la construction du toit de New Collège. Des cottages intacts construits dans le style traditionnel bordent la rivière Eye à Lower Slaughter dont les rives sont reliées par une série de ponts en pierre. Le moulin à blé du 19ème siècle semble un peu anachronique mais le moulin à eau d'origine était peut-être antérieur au premier cadastre (Domesday)

A un demi-mile en amont, le manoir Tudor de Upper Slaughter a été décrit comme l'un des plus beaux des Cotswolds. Plus ruraux que leur voisin, les cottages et fermes se rassemblent près des points de passage de la rivière Eye.

Les deux villages se fondent depuis toujours dans le paysage; le visiteur qui prend le temps de se promener ou qui longe la rivière sur le chemin qui relie les deux villages ressent peut-être encore mieux leur atmosphère.

Bereits 1452 wurde Schiefer aus örtlichen Steinbrüchen nach Oxford transportiert für den Bau des Daches des New College. In Lower Slaughter säumen unberührte, in traditionellem Stil gebaute Cottages den Fluss Eye, dessen Ufer durch zahlreiche Steinbrücken verbunden werden. Die Getreidemühle aus dem 19. Jahrhundert erscheint etwas fehl am Platze, aber die ursprüngliche Wassermühle stammte warscheinlich aus der Zeit vor dem Domesday Book.

Weniger als einen Kilometer stromaufwärts befindet sich Upper Slaughter's Tudor-Gutshaus, das als eines der schönsten in den Cotswolds bezeichnet wird. Pastoraler als ihre Nachbarn, drängen sich die Cottages und Farmen in der Nähe der Furt des Eye.

Beide Orte fügen sich zeitlos in die Landschaft ein und der Besucher, der sich die Zeit nimmt zum Spazierengehen oder den den beiden Gemeinden verbindenden Uferweg entlangzulaufen, weiß ihre Atmosphäre am besten zu schätzen.

1452年という早い時期から、オックスフォード大学の校舎の屋根を葺くために、地元の採石場で切り出したスレートが使われていました。ロウアー スローターには、石造りの橋の架かるアイ川に沿って伝統的な田舎家が当時の姿のまま残っています。19世紀に建てられた水車小屋でさえ、ここでは新しく感じられます。最初の水車小屋はドゥームズデー ブック（1086年）以前の時代にさかのぼるものかもしれません。

上流へ800メートルほど行くと、アッパー スローターがあります。ここのチューダー朝の領主の館はコッツウォルズで最も美しい建築のひとつです。道がアイ川を渡るところに、何軒かの田舎家と牧場からなるひなびた集落があります。

どちらの村も時が止まったかのようにあたりの風景に溶け込んでいます。しばし時を忘れ、川岸に沿って2つの集落の出会うあたりまで散策すると、コッツウォルズの村の雰囲気が堪能できます。

Bourton-on-the-Water

Bourton sells itself as the Venice of the Cotswolds, it is characterised by the river Windrush flowing through the heart of the village, spanned by a series of ornamental low stone bridges. Like Venice, Bourton is a magnet for visitors, drawn by its variety of buildings set near the clear water of the Windrush, and visitor attractions.

Bourton has long been a convenient stopping place for those travelling along the Fosse Way; it was during the Roman occupation that a bridge was first built across the Windrush, and a settlement grew up and became the natural capital of the northern Cotswolds. Saxon remains found nearby in 1931 revealed remains of an upright loom, some of the earliest evidence of the wool processing industry that later became so important to the Cotswolds.

■ **VIC Victoria Street, Bourton-on-the-Water. 01451 820211.**

ATTRACTIONS, EVENTS, AND POINTS OF INTEREST
- Birdland Park – Open all year – 01451 820480. A collection of birds, including penguins, parrots and flamingos, tropical and temperate houses, plus pets corner, picnic area, coffee house and playgrounds.
- Bourton Model Railway. Weekends only between September to May – 01451 820686. Fine working model railways, large shop.
- Cotswold Motoring Museum – Open Mid February to Early December – 01451 821255. Other exhibits include teddy bears, aeroplanes and pedal cars.

- The Dragonfly Maze – Open all year – 01451 822251. Reveal the secret of the Golden Dragonfly in this unique participation experience.
- The Model Village (left) 01451 820467. A 1/9th scale creation of Bourton made of Cotswold stone in 1937, including a model of the model, open all year.
- The Cotswold Perfumery – Open all year – 01451 820698. Explore the origins of perfume. All perfumes are made on the premises. 1 and 2 day courses available to be booked.

Bourton se vend comme étant la Venise des Cotswolds; sa personnalité lui vient de la rivière Windrush qui coule au cœur du village et qui est traversée par une série d'elegants ponts de pierre. Bourton est un aimant pour les visiteurs, conduits là par la variété de ses constructions en pierre établies près des eaux claires de la Windrush, et par les attractions touristiques.

Bourton a longtemps été une étape pour les voyageurs sur la route de Fosse ; ce fut pendant l'occupation romaine qu'un pont fut construit pour la premiere fois au dessus de la Windrush, qu'une agglomeration s'y developpa et devint la capitale naturelle des Cotswolds du nord. Des témoignages du passé saxon mis à jour tout près en 1931 comprennent les restes d'un métier à tisser vertical, l'une des plus anciennes preuves de l'existence d'une industrie de la laine qui devint plus tard si importante pour les Cotswolds.

Bourton vermarktet sich als das Venedig der Cotswolds. Es ist geprägt durch den Fluss Windrush, der durch das Herz des Ortes fließt und von einer Vielzahl dekorativer Steinbrücken überspannt wird. Durch seine Vielfalt an steinernen Gebäuden in der Nähe des klaren Wassers des Windrush und seine Besucherattraktionen ist Bourton ein Magnet für Besucher.

Bourton war schon seit langer Zeit ein günstig gelegener Rastplatz für Reisende am Fosse Way. Es war während der Zeit der römischen Besetzung, als die erste Brücke über den Windrush gebaut wurde und eine Siedlung entstand, die zur natürlichen Hauptstadt der nördlichen Cotswolds wurde. Angelsächsische Überreste, die 1931 in der Nähe gefunden wurden, brachten Überbleibsel eines aufrechten Webstuhls zum Vorschein, einen der frühesten Beweise der wollverarbeitenden Industrie, die später für die Cotswolds so bedeutsam wurde.

ウィンドラッシュ川が村の中心部を流れるバートン オン ザ ウォーターは、コッツウォルズのベニスとして知られています。装飾的な石橋が架かるウィンドラッシュ川の清流のほとりに建ち並ぶさまざまな石造りの家が多くの観光客を集めています。

バートン オン ザ ウォーターは、ローマ時代に最初の橋が建設されて以来、フォッス街道を旅する旅行者が泊まる宿場町として自然に発達し、コッツウォルズ北部の中心地となりました。1931 年にこの近くで発見されたサクソン人の遺跡からはた織機が出土し、のちにコッツウォルズの中心産業となった毛織物が古い時代から存在していたことが証明されました。

Area 4 General

OTHER ATTRACTIONS IN AREA 4

Cotswold Farm Park, Guiting Power – Open middle of February to September, and weekends in October – 01451 850307. Over 50 breeding herds and flocks of some of the country's rarest farm animals. Includes pets corner, touch barn, adventure playground, picnic area, nature trail, café and gift shop.

OTHER PLACES OF INTEREST IN AREA 4

A tour clockwise around Stow-on-the-Wold reveals many picturesque villages: Longborough with fine views towards Moreton; Donnington, site of a famous battle during the English Civil War and today known for the nearby brewery; Broadwell and the Oddingtons; Adlestrop, which was mentioned in a poem by Edward Thomas; Maugersbury and finally Upper and Lower Swell complete the circle.

The Windrush Valley takes you to Temple Guiting, Kineton – beware of the ford – and Guiting Power, before emerging into the water meadows at Naunton, a settlement mentioned in the Doomsday Book. Great and Little Rissington overlook Bourton and the Windrush from the east.

At Bourton, the Windrush Way, a sign-posted walk, leads westwards along the river valley, up over Naunton Downs to Winchcombe. Then, as the Wardens Way and similarly sign-posted, the walk doubles back to the north, alongside Guiting Wood to Guiting Power, Naunton and finally back to Bourton. The Oxfordshire Way starts here, but on an easterly track.

Maugersbury

Cotswold Farm Park

Donnington Brewery

Autres Lieux Intéressants : Région 4

Un tour dans le sens des aiguilles d'une montre autour de Stow-on-the-Wold fait découvrir beaucoup de villages pittoresques ; Longborough avec un beau point de vue sur Moreton ; Donnington, site d'une bataille très connue pendant la guerre civile anglaise et maintenant plus connue pour la brasserie toute proche et pour son élevage de truites ; Broadwell et the Oddingtons, Adlestrop, Maugersbury et enfin Upper et Lower Swell.

La vallée de la Windrush vous emmène à Temple Guiting, Kineton et Guiting Power, avant d'émerger dans les prairies de Naunton. Great et Little Rissington surplombent Bourton et la Windrush à l'est.

A Bourton, la Windrush Way, une promenade clairement signalisée, mène à Winchcombe vers l'ouest en suivant la vallée de la Windrush, en passant par Naunton Downs. Ensuite, devenue la Wardens Way, la promenade revient vers Guiting Power, Naunton et finalement vous ramène à Bourton. Là débute l'Oxfordshire Way, mais vers l'est.

Weitere Sehenswerte Orte – Gebiet 4

Eine Tour im Uhrzeigersinn um Stow-on-the-Wold führt durch viele malerische Dörfer: Longborough mit einer herrlichen Aussicht nach Moreton; Donnington, der Ort einer berühmten Schlacht während des Englischen Bürgerkrieges und heute besser bekannt für seine nahegelegene Brauerei und Forellenfarm; Broadwell und die Oddingtons, Adlestrop, Maugersbury und zuletzt Upper und Lower Swell.

Das Tal des Windrush führt nach Temple Guiting, Kineton und Guiting Power, bevor es in die Flussauen von Naunton mündet. Great und Little Rissington überschauen Bourton und den Windrush von Osten.

In Bourton führt der Windrush Way, ein beschilderter Wanderweg, dem Flusstal entlang nach Westen, über Naunton Downs nach Winchcombe. Dann führt der Weg als Wardens Way zurück nach Guiting Power, Naunton und schließlich nach Bourton, wo der Oxfordshire Way in östlicher Richtung beginnt.

その他の見どころ ― エリア 4

ストウ オン ザ ウォルドを中心に 12 時方向から時計回りに見ていくと、次のような美しい村に出合います。ロングバラー (Longborough) ではモートン方向へすばらしい眺望が楽しめます。ドニントン (Donnington) は清教徒革命時代の有名な古戦場ですが、今日では近くの醸造所とマスの養魚場のほうがよく知られています。このほかブロードウェル (Broadwell)、アドレストロップ (Adlestrop)、オディントン (Oddingtons)、モーガスベリー (Maugersbury)、アッパーおよびロアー スウェル (Upper Swell、Lower Swell) などの村々があります。

ウィンドラッシュ渓谷 (Windrush Valley) は、テンプル ガイティング (Temple Guiting)、キナトン (Kineton)、ガイティング パワー (Guiting Power) の村々を経て、ノーントン (Naunton) の牧草地に至ります。バートン オン ザ ウォーターとウィンドラッシュ川の東側にはグレート リシントン (Great Rissington) とリトル リシントン (Little Rissington) があります。

バートン オン ザ ウォーターを起点として、西に向かって標識の整備された遊歩道、ウィンドラッシュ街道が渓谷沿いにノーントンの牧草地を過ぎてウィンチコムまで伸びています。ウィンチコムで折り返した道はワードンズ街道となって、ガイティング パワー、ノーントンを経由してバートン オン ザ ウォーターに戻ります。ここからは東に向かうオックスフォード街道を歩くこともできます。

Chipping Norton

On the north-eastern fringe of the Cotswolds, the old market town known as 'Chippy' perches at 200 metres, the highest town in Oxfordshire. Chipping derives from *Ceapen*, the medieval term for market, and the source of the town's early wealth. From the 13th century wool was traded here, and by the 15th century the town prospered. Wool merchant John Ashfield paid for dramatic alterations to St Mary's Church in 1485; the slender pillars and clerestory windows above the nave creating one of the finest interiors of any Cotswold church.

Local industrialist William Bliss was instrumental in bringing the railway to Chipping Norton in the 19th century; he needed coal to supply the steam engines at Bliss Mill where tweed was manufactured. The redundant mill still stands on the edge of the town, an imposing stone building now converted for residential use.

'Chippy' continues to be a bustling market town and is one of the few towns in the area to have its own theatre.

ATTRACTIONS, EVENTS, AND POINTS OF INTEREST

- Market Day - Wednesday.
  Farmers' Market - 3rd Saturday each month.
- Chipping Norton Museum – Open Easter to October – 01608 641712. An exhibition of local history.
- A quaint row of Almshouses, built in 1646, lines the cul-de-sac to the church.
- The Castle Mounds are earthworks and the only reminder that this was the site of a substantial castle, built by Ernulf d'Hesdin, a supporter of William the Conqueror.
- The Market Place was first laid out in 1205.
- A Mop Fair, traditionally a fair for the hiring of servants, is held in September.
- The Theatre, Spring Street – Open all year – Box Office 01608 642350.

Sur la frange nord-est des Cotswolds la vieille ville commerçante connue sous le nom de "Chippy" culmine à 200 mètres, c'est la plus haute ville de l'Oxfordshire. Le nom Chipping vient de Ceapen, le mot médiéval qui signifie marché. Des le 13ème siècle la laine se vendait là, et au 15ème siècle la ville était prospère. L'industriel local William Bliss réussit à faire venir le chemin de fer à Chipping Norton au 19ème siècle afin d'acheminer le charbon pour les machines à vapeur des filatures Bliss où on fabriquait du tweed. Les filatures maintenant inutilisées ont été reconverties en habitations.

Chippy est toujours une ville commerçante active, centrée autour de sa place du marché dont le plan a été très peu modifié, et est une des rares villes de la région à avoir son propre théâtre.

Am nordöstlichen Rand der Cotswolds liegt auf 200 Metern Höhe das als „Chippy" bekannte alte Marktstädtchen, die höchstgelegenste Stadt in Oxfordshire. Chipping ist abgeleitet von Ceapen, dem mittelalterlichen Ausdruck für Markt. Seit dem 13. Jahrhundert wurde hier mit Wolle gehandelt, und schon im 15. Jahrhundert prosperierte die Stadt. Der Industrielle William Bliss hat Chipping Norton im 19. Jahrhundert zu einer Eisenbahn verholfen, um die Kohle für die Dampfmaschinen der Bliss-Weberei zu liefern, wo Tweed hergestellt wurde. Die stillgelegte Weberei wurde später zu Wohnungen umgestaltet.

Chippy ist nach wie vor ein beliebtes Marktstädtchen das sich um den Marktplatz konzentriert, dessen Anlage sich im Laufe der Zeit wenig verändert hat. Sie ist eine der wenigen Städte der Gegend mit einem eigenen Theater.

コッツウォルズの北東端に接するチッピング ノートンは、オックスフォードシャーで最も高いところ（標高 200 メートル）にある古い市場町で、「チッピー」という名で親しまれています。チッピングの語源は中世の英語で「市場」を表す「Ceapen」にあります。この町では、13 世紀以降毛織物の市が開かれ、15 世紀まで繁栄しました。19 世紀になって、地元の産業主義者ウィリアム・ブリスの力によって、鉄道がこの町を通るようになり、当時ツイードを生産していたブリス紡績工場（Bliss Mill）では、蒸気機関車に石炭と水を供給していました。この紡績工場は閉鎖後改築され、現在は住宅になっています。

チッピング ノートンは、現在も町の広場を中心に昔のままの姿を残す市場町としてにぎわっています。また、チッピング ノートンには、このあたりの町には珍しい劇場もあります。

Burford

Architectural variety features in the broad street sweeping down the hill towards the river Windrush, half-timbered buildings, their oak beams from nearby Wychwood Forest, mix with the more familiar stone. At the bottom of the street, a medieval bridge built in 1322 crosses the river Windrush near the 15th century church.

Wool and cloth were traded in the main street, and Burford was a leading wool market by 1400. Nearby quarries in Taynton provided high quality stone, widely used locally and further afield (see Lechlade p26). Burford continued to thrive following the demise of the wool trade, its inns offering refreshment to travellers on what became a major coaching route. The George Hotel offered accommodation for King Charles II and Nell Gwyn, while visiting the nearby Bibury races.

■ TIC 33a High Street, Burford OX18 4QA. 01993 823558. www.oxfordshirecotswolds.org

ATTRACTIONS, EVENTS, AND POINTS OF INTEREST
- Market Day - at nearby Carterton on Thursday.
- The Tolsey Museum. – Open April to October, not Mondays, except Bank Holidays. A 16th century merchants meeting place now a museum of local history.
- Cotswold Wildlife Park and Gardens – Open all year – 01993 823006. A 160 acre estate, wide variety of animals, insect and reptile house. Narrow gauge railway, children's farmyard and adventure playground. Restaurant and gift shop.

- Burford Trail. An easy to follow town guide directing you passed the historical sites and buildings is available from the Visitor Information Centre.
- The Dragon Parade is held in July. Local school children dress as dragons and march through the town to commemorate a Saxon battle.
- Levellers Day. An annual remembrance, held in May, of the execution of three men from Cromwell's Army who took a stand for representative democracy.
- Good centre for walking and cycling the Oxfordshire Cotswolds. The Thames Path, Oxfordshire Way, Wychwood Way and many other circular day routes are within easy reach.

Today's Burford has much to offer the visitor including several historic inns, and a stroll along some of the quieter streets will reveal a range of interesting buildings including the 15th century almshouses near the church.

C'est une architecture variée qui se remarque dans la grand-rue qui dévale la colline vers la rivière Windrush, avec des bâtiments partiellement à colombages, dont le bois de chêne de la forêt de Wychwood avoisinante est mêlé à la pierre plus habituelle.

Burford devint un des plus importants marché de la laine vers 1400, vendant laine et tissu dans la rue principale, et elle continua à prospérer malgré la chute du commerce de la laine, ses auberges offrant des rafraîchissements aux voyageurs sur ce qui devint une route très importante. Le George Hôtel abrita le roi Charles II et Nell Gwyn, lorsqu'ils assistèrent aux courses de Bibury.

La Burford d'aujourd'hui a beaucoup de choses à offrir au visiteur, dont de nombreuses auberges chargées d'Histoire, et une promenade dans certaines rues plus calmes permettra de découvrir une série de bâtiments intéressants comme les « almshouses » (logements de bienfaisance pour personnes âgées) du quinzième siècle près de l'église.

Zur architektonischen Vielfalt der breiten Straße, die den Berg zum Fluss Windrush hinunterführt, gehören neben den bekannten Steingebäuden auch Halbfachwerkhäuser mit Eichenbalken aus dem nahengelegenen Wynchwood Forest.

Burford entwickelte sich bis 1400 zu einem führenden Wollmarkt in dessen Hauptstraße Wolle und Tuch gehandelt wurden, und florierte auch später nach dem Niedergang des Wollhandels als Rastplatz an einer der Hauptpreiserouten, wo die Wirtshäuser den Reisenden Erfrischungen anboten. Das George Hotel bot Unterkunft für König Charles II und Nell Gwyn während ihren Besuchen der Pferderennen im nahegelegenen Bibury.

Das heutige Burford hat seinen Besuchern viel zu bieten, einschließlich zahlreicher historischer Wirtshäuser. Ein Spaziergang entlang den ruhigeren Straßen bringt eine Reihe interessanter Gebäude zum Vorschein, wie zum Beispiel die Armenhäuser aus dem 15. Jahrhundert in der Nähe der Kirche.

バーフォードには、広い目抜き通りがウィンドラッシュ川に向かって丘を下るように伸びています。近くのウィッチウッドの森（Wychwood Forest）から切り出した樫を使った木骨構造の家が石造りの家と軒を並べています。

バーフォードは、1400年台までに毛織物の主な市場の１つとなり、毛織物取引きが下火になった後も、駅馬車の通る宿場町として繁栄を続け、旅の疲れをいやす旅行者でにぎわっていました。この町のジョージ ホテル（The George Hotel）には、ビブリーで開かれる競馬を見るために訪れた国王チャールズ２世がネル・グウィンとともに宿泊したこともあります。

今日のバーフォードの静かな通りには、歴史に残るホテルのほか、教会の近くにある15紀の救貧院など、興味深い建物が残っています。

Witney

Witney produced blankets for over 1000 years, their manufacture even surviving the collapse of the Cotswold woollen industry. The waters of the river Windrush were said to have be perfect for scouring woollen cloth, perhaps explaining why Witney blankets were well known for their quality and softness. As early as the 17th century these were exported to America, where native Americans exchanged furs for the red and blue blankets.

Situated on a spur of Cotswold oolite rock extending well into Oxfordshire, Witney has kept its character as a market town despite rapid housing development in recent years. In the centre of the town is Church Green, a large grassed area lined with stone houses and pollarded limes. Overlooked by the massive tower and spire of the 13th century church, the green has remained remarkably timeless, a peaceful haven from the bustle of the nearby market square and streets.

■ **VIC, Town Centre Shop, 3 Welch Way, Witney, OX28 6JH. 01993 775802.**

ATTRACTIONS, EVENTS, AND POINTS OF INTEREST

■ Market Day - Thursday and Saturday.
  Farmers' Market - 4th Friday each month.
■ Cogges Manor Farm Museum – March to October – 01993 772602. A working museum of rural life in the Victorian age, with farm animals, exhibitions and traditional cooking. Café and gift shop.
■ Medieval Bishops Palace – Limited opening – 01865 300557, or the VIC. Ruins of one of the 24 palaces belonging to the Bishop of Winchester, dating from the 12th century, now with it's own visitor's centre.
■ Witney and District Museum – April to October – 01993 775915. Local history, glove making and brewing.
■ The 17th century Butter Cross is at the centre of the Market Place, where sheep were bought and sold as recently as 1950. Just opposite is the Town Hall.
■ Witney Lake and Meadows. A 75-acre country park and nature reserve with a variety of flora and fauna.
■ 'Wool Trail' a trail around Witney indicating the blanket and wool sites

Witney a produit des couvertures pendant plus de 1000 ans, leur fabrication a même survécu à l'effondrement de la laine des Cotswolds. Les eaux de la Windrush sont réputées parfaites pour traiter la laine, ce qui explique peut-être pourquoi les couvertures de Witney étaient connues pour leur qualité et leur douceur. Dès le 17ème siècle des couvertures furent exportées vers l'Amérique, et les indigènes échangèrent des fourrures contre des couvertures rouges et bleues.

Witney a conservé son caractère de ville commerçante malgré un développement rapide des constructions d'habitation. Church Green est une grande pelouse bordée de maisons de pierre et de tilleuls. Surplombée par la tour imposante et l'aiguille de l'église du treizième siècle, la place est restée intemporelle, un havre de paix à coté de l'agitation de la place du marché voisine et des rues commerçantes.

Witney produziert seit über 1000 Jahren Decken, und ihre Herstellung überlebte sogar den Zusammenbruch der Cotswold-Wolle. Das Wasser des Flusses Windrush ist angeblich perfekt zum Waschen des wollenen Tuches, und das erklärt vielleicht warum die Decken aus Witney für ihre Qualität und Weichheit so berühmt sind. Schon im 17. Jahrhundert wurden Decken nach Amerika exportiert, wo die Ureinwohner Felle gegen rote und blaue Decken eintauschten.

Trotz der rapiden Entwicklung des Wohnungsbaus hat Witney seinen Charakter als Marktstädtchen erhalten. Church Green ist eine große Grünfläche, gesäumt von steinernen Häusern und gekappten Linden. Überragt von dem massiven Turm der Kirche aus dem 13. Jahrhundert, ist dieser Anger erstaunlich zeitlos geblieben und stellt neben der Hektik des nahegelegenen Marktplatzes und der Einkaufsstraßen einen friedlichen Zufluchtsort dar.

ウィットニーは1000年も前から毛布を生産しています。コッツウォルズの羊毛産業が衰退した後も、毛布の生産は続いています。ウィンドラッシュ川の水は毛織物を洗うのに理想的であるといわれており、これがウィットニーの毛布の持つ品質と柔らかさの秘密かもしれません。17世紀にはすでに、ここで生産された毛布がアメリカへ輸出されています。当時のアメリカ インディアンは赤や青で染められたウィットニーの毛布を毛皮と物々交換していました。

現在のウィットニーは、急速な住宅開発にもかかわらず、市場町としての性格を残しています。市場や商店街の喧騒のあとで、石造りの家と刈り込まれたライムの木に囲まれた尖塔のそびえる13世紀の教会の緑地帯に座ると、時の流れの止まった別天地に来たかのようです。

Area 5 General

Blenheim Palace

OTHER ATTRACTIONS IN AREA 5

Aston Pottery, Bampton – Open all year. 01993 852031. A working pottery, with award winning shop, coffee house and picnic area.

Blenheim Palace, Woodstock – House open February to November, grounds open all year. Group bookings 01993 815600. The magnificent home of the 12th Duke of Marlborough and birthplace of Sir Winston Churchill. The 2,500 acre park includes a lake, butterfly house, The Marlborough Maze plus shops, cafeterias and a restaurant. Annual events include a flower show, craft fairs, concerts and horse trials.

Charlbury Museum, Charlbury – Limited opening Easter to October – 01608 810709. Featuring local history, traditional crafts and the glove industry.

Chastleton House, Chastleton – Limited opening – 01608 674355. Jacobean mansion built in 1603, where the rules of croquet were codified. The house

includes fine period furniture and a secret room where, it is thought, the Royalist family hid during the Civil War.

North Leigh Roman Villa, North Leigh. A site to the west of Woodstock, excavated in 1813. The remains of buildings can be seen, along with the excellent mosaic pavement.

Oxford Bus Museum, Long Hanborough – Limited opening – 01993 883617. An enthusiast's collection of 40 vehicles from 1915 to 1962.

The Oxfordshire Museum, Woodstock – Open all year – 01993 814106. A celebration of the county's heritage, including the 'Stonesfield Carpet' and glove industry for which Woodstock was famous.

Rollright Stones. North of Chipping Norton are three separate Bronze Age stone erections, the subject of medieval legend.

Rousham House and Gardens, Rousham – Gardens open daily all year 10am - 4.30pm. House open by appointment, 01869 347110. A totally un-commercialised 17th century house with a rare example of a William Kent garden.

Woodstock Textile Trail, Woodstock – The Woodstock Textile Group 01993 814106. See The Blenheim Tapestries, The Woodstock Wallhangings, The Stonesfield Embroidery and The Kneelers

OTHER PLACES OF INTEREST IN AREA 5

The King's Stone

The Oxfordshire Way and river Evenlode meet at Bledington and continue side by side through Shipton and Ascott-under-Wychwood, parting at North Leigh. To the east of Chipping Norton is Enstone and Great, Little and Duns Tews, which featuring an abundance of thatched cottages and quiet lanes leading into the Cherwell Valley. To the south, Charlbury sits astride the Evenlode on the edge of Wychwood Forest, a former Royal hunting ground. The deerskins from these hunts gave rise to the local glove industry.

West of Burford The Barringtons face each other across the Windrush. River walks exist east through Swinbrook and Asthall. The Romans had a settlement here on Akeman Street, their main road linking Cirencester and St Albans. Minster Lovell, known for the 15th century Hall of the Lovell, is the last riverside settlement before the Windrush reaches Witney.

To the south Shilton and Westwell are perfect examples of unspoilt Cotswold villages.

OTHER VICs
- **VIC The Oxfordshire Museum, Park Street, Woodstock. 01993 814106.**
- **VIC, Broad Street, Oxford. 01865 686430.**

Autres Lieux Intéressants : Région 5
L'Oxfordshire Way et la rivière Evenlode se rencontrent à Bledington et continuent pratiquement cote à cote à travers Shipton et Ascott–under- Wychwood jusqu'à North Leigh. Enstone et les pittoresques villages de Great, Little et Duns Tews, a l'est de Chipping Norton, mènent dans la vallée de la Cherwell. Au sud, Charlbury s'étend de part et d'autre de la rivière Evenlode a la lisière de la forêt de Wychwood, une ancienne chasse royale.
A l'ouest de Burford les villages de Barrington se font face sur les deux rives de la Windrush. Il y a des promenades agréables à faire le long de la rivière à l'est en passant par Swinbrook et Asthall. Minster Lovell, un joli village plus connu peut-être pour son monument du 15ème siècle est le dernier lieu d'habitation sur la rivière avant que la Windrush arrive a Witney.
Au sud on trouve Westwell et Shilton, parfaits exemples de villages des Cotswolds intacts, à quelques minutes seulement du tohu-bohu de leurs grands voisins.

Weitere Sehenswerte Orte – Gebiet 5
Der Oxfordshire Way und der Fluss Evenlode treffen sich in Bledington und laufen von dort fast nebeneinander durch Shipton und Ascott-under-Wynchwood nach North Leigh. Enstone und die malerischen Orte Great-, Little- und Duns Tew östlich von Chipping Norton führen in das Tal des Cherwell hinein. Südlich davon, sitzt Charlbury rittlings auf dem Fluss Evenlode am Rande des Wynchwood Forest, einem früheren königlichen Jagdgebiet.
Westlich von Burford liegen sich die Barringtons am Windrush gegenüber. Schöne Flusswanderungen gibt es nach Osten durch Swinbrook und Asthall. Minster Lovell, ein hübsches Dorf, das warscheinlich am besten bekannt ist für die historische Stätte aus dem 15. Jahrhundert, ist die letzte Siedlung am Flussufer bevor der Windrush Witney erreicht.
Nach Süden hin sind Westwell und Shilton perfekte Beispiele unberührter Cotswold-Dörfer, nur Minuten entfernt vom geschäftigen Treiben der größeren Nachbarn.

その他の見どころ ― エリア5
オックスフォード街道とイブンロード川はブレディントン（Bledington）で出合い、その後シプトン（Shipton）とアスコット アンダー ウィッチウッド（Ascott-under-Wychwood）を経由してノース レイ（North Leigh）までほぼ平行に走っています。チッピング ノートンの東には、エンストーン（Enstone）と、グレート チュー（Great Tew）、リトル チュー（Little Tew）、ダンス チュー（Duns Tew）の美しい村々を通り、チェアウェルの谷（Cherwell Valley）に至る道があります。その南には、かつて王家の狩猟場だったウィッチウッドの森に接して流れるイブンロード川をまたいでチャールベリー（Charlbury）があります。
バーフォード（Burford）の西には、ウィンドラッシュ川を挟んで、グレート バーリントン（Great Barrington）とリトル バーリントン（Little Barrington）が向かい合っています。東にはスウィンブルック（Swinbrook）とアストール（Asthall）を通って、15世紀の建築で知られる美しい村ミンスター ラベル（Minster Lovell）に至る気持ちのよい川沿いの遊歩道があります。この後、ウィンドラッシュ川はウィットニーを通り、テームズ川に合流します。
バーフォードの南にあるウェストウェル（Westwell）とシルトン（Shilton）は、昔のコッツウォルズの姿を残す典型的な村です。ここでは、ほんの数分のところにある町の喧騒を忘れさせてくれます。

Bibury

Apart from the numbers of visitors and the influence of cars and coaches, Bibury may have changed little since the poet and artist William Morris described it as the 'most beautiful village in all England.' It is not only the buildings, but the lush valley and the fast flowing clear trout-rich water of the river Coln that help to make Bibury and its neighbour Arlington so attractive

A triple-arched 18th century bridge leads across the river to Arlington, home of a famous row of stone cottages overlooking water meadows. Originally a medieval house and store, a 17th century conversion created tiny cottages to house the weavers who provided cloth for fulling at the nearby Arlington mill. Rack Isle, the meadow in front the cottages, is now managed as a nature reserve but was once used by the weavers for drying wool.

Bibury's centre clusters near the originally Saxon church of St Mary's. The village's 17th century prosperity is reflected among the many stone cottages and houses.

■ **VIC in the Corinium Museum, Park Street, Cirencester, Gloucestershire, GL7 2BX. 01285 654180.**
ATTRACTIONS, EVENTS, AND POINTS OF INTEREST

■ Bibury Trout Farm – Open all year – 01285 740215. One of the oldest trout farms in the country, dating from 1902, with café and shop. Visitors can feed and catch the fish.
■ Arlington Row. This is one of the most photographed Cotswold landmarks.

En dehors du nombre de visiteurs et du trafic, Bibury n'a probablement pas changé depuis que le poète et artiste William Morris l'a qualifié de « plus beau village de toute l'Angleterre ». C'est non seulement les bâtiments mais aussi la vallée luxuriante et les eaux vives riches en truites de la rivière Coln qui rendent Bibury et sa voisine Arlington si attirantes.

Un pont à trois arches du 18ème siècle fait traverser la rivière pour mener à Arlington, connue à cause d'un fameux alignement de cottages. A l'origine c'était une villa médiévale et sa grange qui furent transformés au 17ème siècle en minuscules cottages pour loger les tisserands qui fournissaient la toile à fouler à la filature toute proche. Rack Isle, la prairie devant les cottages, est désormais une réserve naturelle.

Abgesehen von der Anzahl der Besucher und dem Einfluss des Verkehrs hat sich Bibury kaum verändert seitdem es der Poet und Künstler William Morris als das „schönste Dorf in ganz England" beschrieben hat. Es sind nicht nur die Gebäude sondern auch das grüne Tal und das schnell-fließende, klare, forellenreiche Wasser des Flusses Coln, die zur Attraktivität Biburys und des benachbarten Arlington beitragen.

Eine dreibogige Brücke aus dem 18. Jahrhundert führt über den Fluss nach Arlington, der Heimat einer berühmten Reihe von Stein-Cottages. Das ursprüngliche, mittelalterliche Haus mit Speicher wurde im 17. Jahrhundert zu kleinen Cottages für die Weber umgebaut, die das Tuch zum Walken in der nahegelegenen Fabrik herstellten. Rack Isle, das Weideland vor den Cottages, ist heute ein Naturschutzgebiet.

訪れる観光客の数と交通量が増加したことを除けば、バイブリーは、19世紀の詩人でもあり、工芸家でもあるウィリアム・モリスが「英国で最も美しい村」と呼んだときとほとんど変わっていません。バイブリーとその隣村のアーリントン（Arlington）の魅力は、マスの泳ぐ渓流と、青々と茂った谷と、石造りの家とが織り成す調和美でしょう。

コルン川に架かる18世紀に建設された3重のアーチ橋を渡ると、小さな石造りのコッテージが連なる有名なアーリントン　ロー（Arlington Row）を訪れることができます。これはもともとあった中世の農家と納屋を、17世紀に織工の住居として一連の小舎に改築したものです。ここに住む織工が織った布は近くの水車を使って縮充処理（石鹸水溶液などで布をぬらして、機械的にもむ処理）されました。縮充の済んだ布は洗い張りの要領でコッテージの前の草地で干しました。この草地はラック　アイル（Rack Isle）と呼ばれ、現在は自然保護区に指定されています。

Cirencester

This small rural town was once second only to London in size; as the Roman settlement of Corinium Dobunnorum, this was an important administrative centre with temples, a forum and a basilica. Apart from a grass covered amphitheatre and a few sections of wall, little remains of the Roman centre, but the Corinium Museum houses many Roman treasures such as mosaics and fine religious sculptures.

Today's Cirencester has grown around a prosperous medieval wool town; it was the great market of the southern Cotswolds. Cathedral-like St John Baptist Church dominates the market square with its 50 metre tower. The three-storeyed porch, built at the end of the 15th century as an office for the abbey's secular wool business, displays impressive fan vaulting.

Despite its busy market and shops, Cirencester retains much of its historic charm; the market square and side streets reveal old stone buildings including almshouses and weavers cottages, and there is a sense of space in the parks and open spaces in and around the town.

■ **VIC in the Corinium Museum, Park Street, Cirencester, Gloucestershire, GL7 2BX. 01285 655611.**

ATTRACTIONS, EVENTS, AND POINTS OF INTEREST
- Market Days - Monday and Friday.
  Farmers' Market - 2nd and 4th Saturday each month.
  Antique market Fridays.
  Craft market Saturdays.
- New Brewery Arts – Open all year – 01285 657181. A listed craft shop whose resident workers organise workshops for adults and children. The café appears in the Good Café Guide. Regular theatre and musical performances.
- Cirencester Lock Up. A 19th century detention centre for wrongdoers before the advent of the police force.
- Privately owned Cirencester Park hosts polo during the summer and is open every day to walkers.
- Corinium Museum. – Open all year – 01285 655611. An award-winning museum with one of the finest collections and reconstructions of Roman life. Café and restaurant.
- Roman Amphitheatre – Open all year – Grass covered remains to the west of the town.
- St John Baptist church – Open all year – 01285 659317. One of the great Cotswold wool churches.
- The Abbey grounds, between the church and river Churn, is a relaxing recreational area ideal for picnics away from the noise of the town.
- The Cotswold Show and Country Fair is a major celebration of country life, held each year in Cirencester Park, it features aerobatic displays, falconry, sheepdog trials, ferret racing and many craft and antique stalls.
- An Early Music Festival is held every July.
- The open-air swimming pool is open May to September. 01285 653947.

Cette petite ville rurale fut à l'époque romaine la plus grande ville après Londres; sous le nom de Corinium Dobunnorum c'etait un centre administratif important avec ses temples, son forum et sa basilique. En dehors de l'amphithéâtre recouvert d'herbe et quelques parties de mur il ne reste que peu de choses du centre romain, mais on trouve beaucoup de trésors romains au musée Corinium.

La Cirencester d'aujourd'hui s'est développée autour d'une riche cite lainière médiévale, le grand marché des Cotswolds du sud. L'église St John Baptist qui ressemble à une cathédrale domine la place du marché du haut des 50 mètres de sa tour. Malgré son marché et ses magasins actifs, Cirencester a conservé beaucoup de son charme historique ; la place de marché et les rues avoisinantes recèlent de vieilles constructions de pierre dont des almshouses (logement de charité pour personnes âgées) et des maisons de tisserands, et les parcs et les esplanades donnent une impression d'espace.

Dieses kleine ländliche Städtchen war einst als die römische Siedlung Corinium Dobunnorum zweitgrößte Stadt nach London und ein bedeutendes administratives Zentrum mit Tempeln, Forum und Basilika. Abgesehen von einem grasüberwucherten Amphitheater und einigen Segmenten der Stadtmauer ist wenig von diesem römischen Zentrum erhalten geblieben, aber das Corinium Museum beherbergt viele römische Schätze.

Das heutige Cirencester hat sich aus einer prosperierenden mittelalterlichen Woll-Stadt entwickelt, dem großen Markt der südlichen Cotswolds. Der Marktplatz wird von der Kathedrale-artigen Kirche St. John the Baptist mit ihrem 50 Meter hohen Turm dominiert. Trotz des geschäftigen Marktes und der Geschäfte hat Cirencester viel von seinem historischen Charme erhalten. Der Marktplatz und seine Seitenstraßen lassen zahlreiche alte Steingebäude erkennen, unter anderem Armenhäuser und Webercottages; die Parks und das offene Land vermitteln den Eindruck von Weite.

この小さな地方の一都市は、ローマ時代にはコリニウム ドブノルム (Corinium Dobunnorum) と呼ばれ、ロンドンに次いでこの国で第二の大きな植民都市でした。コリニウム ドブノルムは、ローマの植民地行政上重要な役割をはたし、寺院、公共広場 (フォルム)、バシリカなどが建っていました。現在は、草に覆われた円形劇場や城壁の一部を除いて、遺跡は残っていません。しかし、サイレンセスターのコリニアム博物館 (Corinium Museum) を訪れれば、この時代の多くの優れた遺物を見ることができます。

現代のサイレンセスターは、中世に繁栄したコッツウォルズ南部の毛織物の大市場を持つ町を土台にしています。洗礼者型ヨハネ教会の高さ 50 メートルの尖塔が市場を見下ろすように聳え立っています。市場や商店でにぎやかなサイレンセスターですが、町のあちらこちらに歴史の面影がよく残されているので、市場の開かれる広場や裏通りを歩くと、教貧院や機織り場などの古い石造りの建物に出合います。公園や空き地にもゆったりとした空間が感じられます。

Lechlade

The Thames valley meets the Cotswolds in Lechlade, where the fine 15th century church of St Lawrence and many of the town houses are built of Cotswold stone. Yet historically Lechlade looked to the river Thames for prosperity. Trade came west from London, and Taynton stone was returned by boat for Windsor Castle, the re-building of St Paul's Cathedral after the Great Fire of London, as well as to Oxford for the colleges. Lechlade is still associated with the river, being the highest navigable point on the Thames. Commercial river traffic has gone but this is a popular mooring place for leisure craft and visitors can hire small boats to explore the river, or enjoy a stroll along a section of the Thames Path. Two Cotswold rivers, the Coln and the Leach, join the Thames here, and the now redundant Thames and Severn Canal once branched off west to Stroud.

- VIC in the Corinium Museum, Park Street, Cirencester, Gloucestershire, GL7 2BX. 01285 655611
- VIC 33a High Street, Burford OX18 4QA. 01993 823558. www.oxfordshirecotswolds.org

ATTRACTIONS, EVENTS, AND POINTS OF INTEREST
- Market day - Wednesday at nearby Fairford.
- Lechlade Trout Fishery – Open all year – 01367 253266. Fly-fishing and, October to March, pike lake.
- The sculpture of Father Thames made for the Great Exhibition of 1851, is at St John's Lock.
- Ha'penny Bridge built in 1792 was so named for the amount of toll charged.
- The walk alongside St Lawrence Church inspired the poet Shelley to write *Summer Evening in a Churchyard* and is named Shelley's walk.
- The Trout Inn was once St John's priory, where medieval monks served refreshments to travellers as they crossed the Thames, 01367 252313. Boats may be hired from here for trips along the Thames. Contact 01793 727083.

La vallée de la Tamise arrive dans les Cotswolds à Lechlade dont l'élégante église St Lawrence du 15ème siècle et de nombreuses maisons sont construit en pierre des Cotswolds. A l'origine Lechlade dépendait de la Tamise qui lui amenait les marchandises de Londres, et qui permettait d'acheminer la pierre de Taynton jusqu'à Oxford et Londres pour être utilisée dans beaucoup de constructions connues dont plusieurs collèges d'Oxford et le château de Windsor.

Lechlade est toujours associée à la rivière, puisque la Tamise n'est navigable que jusqu'à cet endroit en amont. Il n'y a plus de trafiic commercial, mais c'est un mouillage apprécié pour la navigation de plaisance et les touristes peuvent y louer de petits bateaux pour explorer la rivière ou bien prendre plaisir à faire une promenade sur le chemin de halage de la Tamise.

Das Themsetal und die Cotswolds treffen in Lechlade zusammen, dessen prächtige St. Lawrence Kirche aus dem 15. Jahrhundert wie auch viele der Häuser in der Stadt aus Cotswold-Stein gebaut sind. Historisch war Lechlade von der Themse abhängig, die Gewerbe aus London brachte und Taynton-Stein nach Oxford und in die Hauptstadt lieferte für den Bau vieler bekannter Gebäude, einschließlich verschiedener Colleges in Oxford und Windsor Castle.

Lechlade ist noch immer mit dem Fluss verbunden und ist der höchste schiffbare Punkt der Themse. Der kommerzielle Schiffsverkehr wurde eingestellt, aber Lechlade ist ein beliebter Anlegeplatz für Freizeitboote, und die Besucher können sich kleine Boote ausleihen um den Fluss zu erkunden oder einen Spaziergang entlang des Themse-Weges genießen.

コッツウォルド丘陵とテームズ峡谷とが出合うところにあるレッチレードには、15 世紀に建てられたセント ローレンス教会があります。この教会にも、たち並ぶ家々の多くにもコッツウォルズの石が使われています。レッチレードは歴史的にはテームズ川を利用したロンドンやオックスフォードとの交易で栄えました。レッチレードから積み出されたテイントン(Taynton)産の石材はオックスフォード大学の校舎やウィンザー城など、多くの有名な建築に使用されています。

レッチレードはテームズ川のボートが通行可能な最高点にあるため、商業的な河川交通が途絶えた現在でも、レジャー用ボートの保留地として人気があります。小型の川船を借りてテームズ川を遊覧したり、川沿いの遊歩道(Thames Path)をのんびりと歩くのはいかがでしょう。

Area 6 General

OTHER ATTRACTIONS IN AREA 6

Barnsley House Garden, Barnsley – Limited opening – 01285 740000. Noteworthy gardens and house, now operated as an hotel and restaurant

Buscot Park, Buscot – Limited opening – Pleasant Adams style mansion, dating from 1780, set in a 55-acre park. A National Trust site. 01367 240932

The Butts Farm, South Cerney – Easter to October – 01285 862224. A working farmstead with hands on experiences.

Cerney House Gardens, North Cerney – Limited opening Easter to September – 01285 831300. A secret garden overlooking the Churn Valley.

Cotswold Water Park and Keynes Country Park, Ashton Keynes – Open all year – 01285 868096. 133 lakes comprise Britain's largest water park. Water sports include sailing, windsurfing, jet skiing and angling. Plus nature walks, bird watching, golf, children's beach, barbeques and camping.

Cotswold Woollen Weavers, Filkins – Open all year – 01367 860660. An interesting working mill, with shop, exhibition gallery and tearoom.

The Great Barn at Great Coxwell is one of the best surviving tithe barns from the 13th century.

Kelmscott Manor, Kelmscott – Limited opening – 01367 252486. Owned by the Society of Antiquaries of London the manor was the country home of William Morris. Licensed restaurant, exhibition and shop.

The source of the Thames is located south west of Cirencester at Kemble.

Swinford Museum, Filkins – Limited opening – 01367 860504. An exhibition of 19th century domestic, trade and craft tools.

OTHER PLACES OF INTEREST IN AREA 6

The Coln valley to the south of Fossebridge contains a string of delightful villages. Coln St Dennis, Calcot, Coln Rogers, Winson and Ablington all lie beside the river Coln, before it arrives at Bibury. The Coln continues through Coln St Aldwyns, Quenington and on to Fairford, the latter noted for its 15th century church, whose 28 medieval stained glass windows are the only complete set remaining in a British Parish church. To the east the river Leach links other charming villages from Northleach to Eastleach Turville and Eastleach Martin and Lechlade.

North of Cirencester the river Churn twists alongside the A435 from Cheltenham. Take time to deviate off the main road and discover more hidden delights,

Kelmscott Manor

Coln St Dennis

Elkstone and the Duntisbournes to the west and Chedworth, Rendcomb and North Cerney in the east. South the isolated valleys disappear giving way to the water parks surrounding Ashford Keynes.

OTHER VICs
■ **VIC Regency Circus, Swindon. 01793 466454**

Autres Lieux Intéressants – Région 6
Il y a toute une chaîne de délicieux villages dans la vallée de la Coln entre Fossebridge et Bibury : Coln St Denis, Calcot, Coln Rogers et Winson. La vallée se poursuit à travers d'autres charmant villages, Coln St Aldwyns et Quenington avant d'arriver à Fairford, remarquable par son église du iséme siécle dont la série de vitraux du moyen age est le seul ensemble complet de vitraux d'église paroissiale a avoir survécu.
    A l'est la rivière Leach relie Northleach et Lechlade en passant par les villages intacts d'Eastleach Turville et Eastleach Martin.
    Au nord de Cirencester, la A435 venant de Cheltenham suit la vallée de la Churn dans laquelle on trouve d'autres joyaux : Elkstone, The Duntisbournes, Chedworth, Rendcomb et North Cerney. Au sud les vallées isolées disparaissent et font place aux plans d'eau entourant Ashford Keynes.

Weitere Sehenswerte Orte – Gebiet 6
Im Tal des Coln zwischen Fossebridge und Bibury liegt eine Kette von reizenden Dörfern: Coln St Denis, Calcot, Coln Rogers und Winson. Das Tal führt weiter durch andere reizvolle Orte, Coln St Aldwyns und Quenington, bevor es Fairford erreicht. Letzteres ist erwähnenswert für seine kirche aus dem is. Jahrhundert deren 28 Buntalasfenster der einzige verliebene komplette Satz mittelalterlicher fenster in einer britischen Germeinderkirche sind.
    Nach Osten hin fließt der Fluss Leach, der Northleach und Lechlade verbindet, durch die unberührten Orte Eastleach Turnville und Eastleach Martin.
    Nördlich von Cirencester folgt die Landstraße A435 von Cheltenham kommend dem Churn-Tal, in dem weitere versteckte Schätze – Elkstone, die Duntisbournes, Chedworth, Rendcomb und North Cerney – zu finden sind. Nach Süden hin lösen sich die einsamen Täler auf und geben Raum für die Wasser-Parks, die Ashford Keynes umgeben.

その他の見どころ ― エリア 6
フォックスブリッジ（Fossebridge）とビブリー（Bibury）の間のコルン川沿いの渓谷には、コルン セント デニス（Coln St Denis）、カルコット（Calcot）、コルン ロジャース（Coln Rogers）、ウィンソン（Winson）、アブリントン（Ablington）の村々が気持ちの良いたたずまいを見せています。渓谷はさらにコルン セント アルドウィンズ（Coln St Aldwyns）、ケニントン（Quenington）などの村々を通り、フェアフォード（Fairford）まで続いています。フェアフォードは、聖書の物語を描いた美しいステンドグラスを持つ15世紀の教会で有名です。中世のステンドグラスの窓がすべて完全な形で残っている教区教会は、英国でここしかありません。
    コルン川の東を流れるリーチ川は、ノースリーチとレッチレードをつないでいます。途中には昔ながらの姿を残すイーストリーチ タービル（Eastleach Turvile）とイーストリーチ マーチン（Eastleach Martin）があります。
    サイレンセスターから A435 号線を北に向かうと、エルクストン（Elkstone）、ダンティスボーンズ（Duntisbournes）、チェドワース（Chedworth）、レンドコム（Rendcomb）、ノース サーニー（North Cerney）などの村々が隠された チャーン渓谷（Churn Valley）を通ってチェルトナムへ行くことができます。サイレンセスターの南は平野が開け、アシュフォード ケインズ（Ashford Keynes）の周辺にはいくつかの水上公園があります。

Dursley

Nestling among the steep slopes of the fragmented western escarpment, Dursley lies beneath the Cotswold edge and along with its close neighbour Cam, was a centre for cloth making. One factory in Cam still manufactures cloth for snooker table covers.

Dursley retains some architectural features such as the arcaded market hall, built in 1738 on the site of the old butter cross, and the town still has an atmosphere of charm and tradition.

The Cotswold Way passes through Dursley, this stretch between Cam Long Down and North Nibley is one the most strenuous part of the route but offers breathtaking views along the indented, wooded escarpment and down towards the Severn estuary.

Situated on fields beside the Severn at Slimbridge, is the newly extended Wildfowl and Wetlands Trust Centre, founded by the late Sir Peter Scott in 1946 to protect the vast numbers of wildfowl that over-winter on the rich feeding grounds.

■ **Information from Dursley Pool, Castle Street, Dursley. 01453 546441**
■ **TIC 33 Church Street, Tetbury, Glos. 01666 503552**

ATTRACTIONS, EVENTS, AND POINTS OF INTEREST
■ Farmers' Market - 2nd Saturday in each month (March to December.
■ Dursley was mentioned in the Doomsday Book and had become a market town by the 1470's.
■ The Market Hall is still used by traders today.
■ A statue of Queen Anne faces the church of St James the Great, which she helped to rebuild by way of a national appeal. Much of the church is 500 years old.
■ A local town trail guides you through the historic streets where many of the original buildings have been sympathetically restored.
■ Slimbridge Wetland Centre, WWT Slimbridge, Bowditch, Slimbridge Gloucestershire 01453 891900

Dursley s'étend aux pieds des bords escarpes des Cotswolds et avec sa voisine Cam était un centre de fabrication de toile ; il y a encore une usine à Cam qui fabrique de la toile pour les uniformes de parade et les revêtements de tables de billard. La modernisation a laissé peu de choses de la ville ancienne sauf par exemple la halle et ses arcades, construite en 1738, et Dursley est encore une ville de charme et de tradition.

Le Cotswold Way passe par Dursley et le passage entre Cam Long Down et North Nibley est la partie la plus difficile de la route et offre des vues à couper le souffle. A coté de la Severn se trouve le Wildfowl and Wetland Trust Centre de Slimbridge, récemment agrandi, qui fut fondé en 1946 par Sir Peter Scott pour protéger les nombreux canards, cygnes et oies qui hivernent sur ces terres riches en nourriture.

Dursley liegt unterhalb der Cotswold-Kante, und zusammen mit dem benachbarten Cam war es ein Zentrum der Tuchherstellung. Eine Fabrik in Cam fertigt noch heute Tuch für Galauniformen und Bezüge für Snookertische. Die Modernisierung hat wenig von der ursprünglichen Stadt übriggelassen, dennoch hat Dursley einige seiner Grundzüge erhalten, wie zum Beispiel die 1738 erbauten Marktarkaden, und ist nach wie vor eine Stadt mit Charme und Tradition.

Der Cotswold Way führt durch Dursley, und das Stück zwischen Cam Long Down und North von Nibley ist der anstrengenste Teil der Route und bietet atemberaubende Aussichten. Am Severn gelegen ist das kürzlich erweiterte Wildfowl und Wetlands Trust Centre in Slimbridge, das 1946 von Sir Peter Scott gegründet wurde um die riesige Anzahl von Gänsen, Enten und Schwänen zu schützen, die in den reichhaltigen Nahrungsgründen überwintern.

コッツウォルド丘陵の南西端に接するダースレイは、隣町のカム（Cam）とともに毛織物生産の中心地でした。カムでは、現在も礼装の生産やスヌーカやビリヤード テーブルに張るビロードが生産されています。近代化のために、創建時のダースレイの姿はほとんど残っていませんが、1729 年に建設された市場のアーケードなどに、この町の伝統と魅力を感じることができます。

ダースレイを通るコッツウォルド街道は、カム ロング ダウン（Cam Long Down）とノース ニブリー（North Nibley）との間の区間が最も急峻で、息をのむようなすばらしい景観が開けています。セバーン川左岸のスリムブリッジ（Slimbridge）には、1946 年にピーター・スコット卿によりここで冬を越すカモ、ガチョウ、ハクチョウなどの水鳥を保護するために創設された「野鳥および湿原トラスト センター」（Wildfowl and Wetlands Trust Centre）があり、最近拡張されました。

Tetbury

Tetbury retains much of the character of a market town of the 17th and 18th centuries. As a centre for Cotswold wool it became prosperous, but lack of adequate water led to a decline by the 19th century. At its hub is the Market House, built in 1655 it is supported by three rows of stout pillars and is still used for markets on Wednesdays and Saturdays. Near the market hall is the Jacobean style Snooty Fox Hotel, rebuilt with entertainment of the local Beaufort Hunt in mind. St Mary's church with its tall elegant spire was built in the late 18th century in Gothic style.

Prosperity is evident in the locality, due in part to the proximity of Highgrove, the Prince of Wales' estate, and Gatcombe, home of the Princess Royal. The emblem of three feathers is displayed in several local businesses, indicating they are 'by appointment to HRH the Prince of Wales'. The town has built up an international reputation as an antique centre and has many other specialist shops.

- **TIC 33 Church Street, Tetbury. 01666 503552**

ATTRACTIONS, EVENTS, AND POINTS OF INTEREST
- Market Day - Wednesday and Saturday.
- Police Bygones Museum – Open all year - 9am - 3pm Monday to Friday – 01666 504670. The old police cells house a collection of relics of Cotswold law enforcement. Free admission.
- Westonbirt Arboretum – 0300 067 4890 – Open all year – 3 miles south west of Tetbury. Founded in 1829 it is now one of Europe's finest collections with 18,000 trees spread across 600 acres. Spectacular displays of flowering Rhododendrons and autumn leaf colour. Gift shop, plant centre and restaurant.
- Over twenty antique centres, with more than fifty dealers.
- The Chipping Steps. The steep cobbled steps and weavers' cottages retain a medieval atmosphere.
- Church of St. Mary the Virgin. One of the finest Georgian Gothic churches, with the fourth highest spire in the country.
- Gumstool Hill. One of Tetbury's oldest streets, today famous for the annual woolsack races and Street Fayre, held every Spring Bank Holiday Monday.
- The Pilgrims Way is a round trip of about 15 miles, linking Tetbury with 6 local villages and their historical importance to worship.

Tetbury a conservé une grande part du caractère de la ville commerçante du 17ème et 18ème siècle. Elle devint une ville prospère grâce à la laine des Cotswolds mais l'absence d'eau adéquate causa son déclin. A son centre on peut voir la Market House ; construite en 1655 elle est soutenue par trois rangées de piliers massifs et est encore utilisée pour les marchés de nos jours. A proximité se trouve le Snooty Fox Hotel de style Jacobée, reconstruit avec en tête l'attraction de la chasse locale « Beaufort Hunt ».
La prospérité locale est visible, due en partie à la proximité de Highgrove, propriété du Prince de Galles, et de Gatcombe, résidence de la Princesse Royale. L'emblème aux trois plumes est affiche dans plusieurs entreprises locales indiquant qu'elles sont « fournisseurs officiels de son Altesse Royale le Prince de Galles ».

Tetbury hat viel vom Charakter eines Marktstädtchens aus dem 17. und 18. Jahrhundert erhalten. Als ein Zentrum für Cotswold-Wolle wurde es zu einer wohlhabenden Stadt; der Mangel an ausreichend Wasser führte jedoch später zum Niedergang. In seinem Zentrum befindet sich das Market House, das 1655 gebaut wurde und von drei Reihen kräftiger Säulen gestützt wird. Es wird noch heute als Markt genutzt. In der Nähe liegt das im jacobeanischen Stil erbaute Snooty Fox Hotel das zum Entertainment der örtlichen Beaufort-Jagd wiedererrichtet wurde.
Der örtliche Wohlstand ist augenscheinlich, zum Teil sicherlich begründet durch die Nähe von Highgrove, dem Landsitz des Prince of Wales, und Gatcombe, dem Haus der Princess Royal. Das Emblem der drei Federn ist in etlichen örtlichen Geschäften zu sehen und bringt zum Ausdruck, dass sie Hoflieferanten für HRH the Prince of Wales sind.

テトベリーには 17〜18 世紀の市場町の姿がよく残っています。この町はコッツウォルドの毛織物の中心地として一時は繁栄していましたが、水に乏しい地形のためにその後衰退していきました。町の中心にある 1655 年建設の3列の太い柱によって支えられたマーケット ハウス(Market House)は、現在でも市場として利用されています。すぐそばにあるジャコビアン様式の「きざなキツネ」という意味の「スヌーティ フォックス ホテル」(Snooty Fox Hotel)は、地元のボーフォート公爵の狩猟会の利用を念頭において改築されたものです。
プリンス オブ ウェールズ(チャールズ皇太子)の所領であるハイグローブ(Highgrove)や、プリンセス ロイヤル(アン王女)の住むガットコム(Gatcombe)に近いテトベリーの豊かさは一目瞭然です。地元の商店のなかには、チャールズ皇太子殿下御用達の店であることを表す 3 本の羽を組み合わせた紋章を表示しているところもあります。

Malmesbury

Malmesbury, a Wiltshire market town of great atmosphere, is distinctly different from other Cotswold towns. It lies on the southern edge of the Area of Outstanding Natural Beauty. It is reputed to be the oldest borough in England, receiving its Royal Charter from Alfred the Great in 880 A.D.

This was one of the early centres of Christianity in Britain, with a monastery established in 640. The town today is still dominated by the imposing remains of its Norman Abbey, noted for the richly carved south porch. The Saxon King Athelstan, the first king of England, is said to be buried here and is remembered in a 14th century monument.

During the 19th century silk was woven here, in mills beside the river Avon. In earlier times it was an important centre for the weaving of wool, and even the abbey was used as a weaving shed following the dissolution of the monasteries.

The town is a rewarding place to visit, with many old buildings, the remains of the town walls and its streets sloping down to the river Avon.

■ **TIC Town Hall, Cross Hayes. 01666 823748**

ATTRACTIONS, EVENTS, AND POINTS OF INTEREST
- Abbey House Gardens – Open March to October – 01666 827650. Five acres of gardens privately owned since 1539, once formed part of the Benedictine Monastery.
- Athelstan Museum – Open all year – 01666 829258. Located in the Town Hall, the museum reflects local history with exhibits of coins, lace making, archaeology, costume, bicycles and The Malmesbury Railway. Travelling exhibitions are a regular feature.
- Malmesbury Abbey – Open all year – Although only a small proportion of the once magnificent Abbey remains, it dominates the skyline for miles around.
- Flying Monk. In the 11th century Eilmer Monk is reputed to have flown down the High Street and despite breaking both legs lived to a healthy old age.
- Malmesbury Carnival – Events, funfair, processions, fete and ball, are held during the last two weeks of August.
- Malmesbury Jazz Festival. Ticket line 01666 824918. Held mid September in venues throughout the town.
- Malmesbury River Walk. Established by the Civic Trust, it connects public and private footpaths along two branches of the river Avon.
- Malmesbury Town Walls. Constructed on the line of early Saxon defences built in response to the threat of a Viking invasion, they were extended during the 12th and 13th centuries and later during the Civil War. Major restoration work is currently in progress.
- The Market Cross, one of the finest in the country, was built around 1490 during the reign of Henry VII.

Malmesbury est une ville commerçante du Wiltshire dotée de beaucoup de caractère et située sur la bordure sud des Cotswolds. Elle revendique le titre de plus ancien « Bourg » d'Angleterre, ce qui lui a été octroyé par une Charte Royale d'Alfred le Grand en 924.

Ce fut l'un des premiers centre Chrétien de Grande-Bretagne, un monastère s'étant établi ici vers 640. Les ruines d'une imposante abbaye Normande dominent encore la ville et la campagne alentour. On dit que le roi saxon Athelstan, premier roi d'Angleterre, y est enterré.

Pendant le 19ème siècle on tissait la soie dans les filatures installée sur l'Avon et auparavant on y tissait la laine. L'abbaye elle-même servit d'atelier de tissage après la dissolution des monastères.

Malmesbury, am Südrand der Cotswolds gelegen, ist ein Wiltshire Marktstädtchen mit besonderer Atmosphäre. Es erhebt Anspruch darauf, die älteste Stadtgemeinde in England zu sein, die eine Royal Charter von Alfred dem Großen im Jahre 924 erhalten hat.

Es war eines der frühesten christlichen Zentren in Britannien mit einem etwa 640 A.D. gegründeten Kloster. Die Überreste der gewaltigen normannischen Abtei dominieren noch heute die Stadt und ihre Umgebung. Der angelsächsische König Athelstan, der erste König von England, ist angeblich hier beerdigt.

Während des 19. Jahrhunderts wurden in den Fabriken am Avon Seide gesponnen, und in früheren Zeiten war es ein Zentrum für das Weben von Wolle. Sogar die Abtei wurde nach der Auflösung der Klöster als Halle zum Weben genutzt.

コッツウォルズの南に接するウィルトシャーにある市場町マルムズベリーは、924 年にアルフレッド大王の勅許を得た英国最古の自治都市です。

マルムズベリーは、英国で最も古いキリスト教の中心地の 1 つで、640 年頃には修道院が建設されました。現在でもノルマン朝にさかのぼる修道院があたりを睥睨しています。イングランド初代の王となったサクソン王アセルスタンは、この地に埋葬されたといわれています。

19 世紀にはエーボン川のほとりで絹織物が生産され、それ以前には毛織物が生産されていました。16 世紀に修道院が解散された後は、修道院さえも毛織物工場として利用されていました。

Area 7 General

OTHER ATTRACTIONS IN AREA 7

Berkeley Castle, Berkeley – April to October – 01453 810303. Built in 1117 and home to 24 generations of the Berkeley family. Collections of furniture, paintings and silver, Elizabethan gardens and Butterfly House.

Chavenage House, near Tetbury – Limited opening May to September – 01666 502329. Historic privately owned Elizabethan House with relics from the Civil War. A family member usually conducts guided tours.

Hodges Barn, Shipton Moyne – Limited opening – Gardens surround a 15th century dovecote.

Jack Russell Gallery, Chipping Sodbury – phone for an appointment – 01454 329583. The famous English cricketer displays his exceptional talent as an artist.

Jenner Museum, Berkeley. April to September. 01453 810631. The home of Dr Edward Jenner, the discoverer of the smallpox vaccine.

Owlpen Manor, near Dursley – April to September. 01453 860261. Impressive historic manor house tucked away in a secluded valley with many unique artefacts, haunted room and Cyder House restaurant.

Newark Park, Ozleworth – Limited opening April to September – 01453 842644. A Tudor hunting lodge built in 1790. A National Trust site.

Rodmarton Manor – Limited opening between May and August – near Tetbury. The English Arts and Crafts movement at its best with beautifully kept gardens 01285 841442.

Ruskin Mill, Nailsworth – Open all year – 01453 837500. Arts and crafts centre, café and working waterwheel.

Tyndale Monument. North Nibley – Open all year. An 111ft monument to the translator of the bible. Keys are available by arrangement.

Uley Tumulus, to the north of Dursley, is an ancient burial site also known as Hetty Peglar's Tump. An ancient hill fort exists to the south with stunning views

The Wildfowl and Wetlands Trust, Slimbridge – Open all year – 01453 891900. The late Sir Peter Scott, who made it a leading centre for bird and wetland conservation, founded the centre. The recently refurbished Visitor Centre offers excellent facilities.

Wotton-under-Edge Heritage Centre – Open all year – 01453 521541. Intriguing artefacts, photographs and pictures of the local district.

The Wildfowl and Wetlands Trust

OTHER PLACES OF INTEREST IN AREA 7

Nailsworth sits at the foot of Minchinhampton Common, the two joined by the steep Nailsworth ladder, a road with a 1 in 2 gradient. Scenic valleys lead in every direction; through Avening to Tetbury, west to Dursley through Nympsfield, the latter easily located by the nearby wind turbine. The deep wooded valleys extend to Dursley, the Cotswold Escarpment and south towards Wotton-under-Edge, through the delightful villages of Uley, Ozleworth, Kingscote, (where in 1788 Catherine Kingscote married Dr Edward Jenner) and Leighterton whose restored church still displays original medieval features.

West is the thriving market town of Chipping Sodbury. Nearby Badminton hosts the famous annual Horse Trials and south of the M4 is another 'must see' village, Castle Combe. It boasts a skidpan, kart racing and was the setting for the 1966 film, Doctor Doolittle. Bath is just 10 miles south, the southern end of The Cotswold Way.

OTHER TICs

- TIC Bridgwater House, 2 Terrace Walk, Bath. 01225 614420
- Wildwalk, At-Bristol, Harbourside 0117 915 100
- TIC Regency Circus, Swindon. 01793 466454
- TIC The Clock Tower, Chipping Sodbury. 01454 326336

Autres Lieux Intéressants : Région 7
Nailsworth est installée au pied de Minchinhampton Common. Des vallées magnifiques en partent de tous cotés : vers Tetbury en passant par Avening ; à l'ouest vers Dursley en passant par Nympsfield et au sud des vallées forestières profondes s'étendent jusqu'à Wotton-under-Edge, en passant par les délicieux villages de Uley, Ozleworth et Kingscote ou en 1788 Catherine Kingscote épousa le Dr Edward Jenner, l'inventeur du vaccin contre la variole.
À l'ouest on trouve une autre ville commerçante florissante, Chipping Sodbury. Badminton tout à coté est le lieu des fameux concours annuels de chevaux et au sud de la M4 il y a encore un autre village à ne pas manquer, Castle Coombe. Il est fier de ses circuits de glisse et de karting, et a été le décor du film Docteur Doolittle de 1966. Bath à 10 miles au sud, est à l'extrémité sud du Cotswold Way.

Weitere Sehenswerte Orte – Gebiet 7
Nailsworth liegt am Fuße des Minchinhampton Common. Malerische Täler führen in alle Richtungen; durch Avening nach Tetbury; nach Westen durch Nympsfield und nach Süden erstrecken sich die tiefen bewaldeten Täler nach Wotton-under-Edge, durch die reizvollen Dörfer Uley, Ozleworth und Kingscote, wo 1788 Catherine Kingscote Dr. Edward Jenner, den Entdecker der Pockenimpfung, heiratete.
Im Westen liegt ein weiteres florierende Marktstädtchen, Chipping Sodbury. Das nahegelegene Badminton richtet die berühmten alljährlichen Horse Trials aus, und gleich südlich der Autobahn M4 liegt ein weiteres Dorf, das man gesehen haben muss - Castle Coombe. Es rühmt sich mit einem Schleuderkurs und einer Go-Kart Rennstrecke und war 1966 Drehort für den Film Doctor Doolittle. Bath liegt 16 km südlich, am südlichen Ende des Cotswold Way.

その他の見どころ — エリア 7
ミンシンハンプトン コモン (Minchinhampton Common) のふもとの町ネイルズワース (Nailsworth) からは、どの方面に向かっても美しい谷が続いています。東には、エイブニング (Avening) からテトベリーに続く谷。西には、ニンプスフィールド (Nympsfield) を経てダースレイに至る谷。また、南のウォットン アンダー エッジ (Wotton-under-Edge) まで広がる谷間の森にはウーリイ (Uley)、オズルワース (Ozleworth)、キングスコート (Kingscote) などの心地よい村々があります。キングスコートは、種痘法の創始者であるエドワード・ジェンナーが 1788 年にキャサリン・キングスコートと結婚したことで知られています。
コッツウォルズの西には、にぎやかな市場町チッピング ソドベリー (Chipping Sodbury) があります。そのそばのバドミントン (Badminton) は、年に 1 度開催されるバドミントン馬術大会 (Badminton Horse Trials) で有名です。高速道路 M4 号線の南側にあるカッスル クーム (Castle Coombe) もぜひ訪れたい村です。スキッド運転練習場とゴーカート競技場があり、1966 年には映画「ドリトル先生不思議な旅」の撮影舞台にもなっています。ローマ時代の浴場で有名なバス (Bath) はコッツウォルド街道の遊歩道の南端から 16 キロほどのところにあります。

Thanks and acknowledgements.

Picture of Blenheim Palace by kind permission of His Grace the Duke of Marlborough.

Grateful thanks to the staff of all Tourist and Visitor Information Centres throughout the Cotswolds, for their kind cooperation and assistance.

All material Copyright © Chris Andrews Publications Ltd 2019.

Published by Chris Andrews Publications Ltd, 15 Curtis Yard, North Hinksey Lane, Oxford OX2 0LX. www.cap-ox.co.uk

Photographs from The Oxford Picture Library: Chris Andrews and Angus Palmer.

Text by Fiona Danks, Angus Palmer

Edited by Chris Andrews.

Revised and updated 2011, 2019 by V C Andrews.

Design by Mike Brain Graphic Design Limited.

Front cover picture – Burford.

Back cover picture – Bourton on the Water.